Staffordshire Hanging Offences

CAPITAL CRIMES

Ros Prince

Churnet Valley Books

PUBLISHED BY

CHURNET VALLEY BOOKS

43 Bath Street Leek
Staffordshire

© Rosalind Prince 1994

ISBN 1897949 08 1

Staffordshire Hanging Offences

as compiled from the original records by

Ros Prince

with some illustrations by
Sally Richardson

For Steve

and the rest of my friends in Staffordshire's

"Thin blue line."

INTRODUCTION

This book developed from "Some Staffordshire Murders", which I wrote for the County Library Service. Whilst conducting my research I was surprised to discover the wide variety of crimes which carried the death penalty in previous centuries.

Murder was an obvious capital crime - but forging a document? passing a 'screeve'? incest? bestiality? rioting? Each of these crimes could take the perpetrator to the gallows. The execution would be watched by hundreds, if not thousands, of fellow Staffordshire residents, some of whom were no doubt guilty of similar offences which remained undiscovered and who were mightily glad that it was not themselves up there.

Some of the post mortem reports, confessions and descriptions of executions which are quoted in the text make pretty gruesome reading, so this is not a book for the faint hearted!

THE COUNTY OF STAFFORD

Locations of offences are shown in bold capitals with chapter numbers alongside.

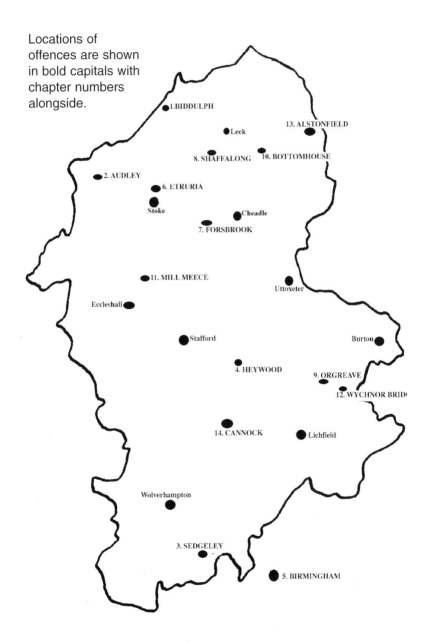

1. BIDDULPH

Leek

13. ALSTONFIELD

8. SHAFFALONG   10. BOTTOMHOUSE

2. AUDLEY

6. ETRURIA

Stoke

Cheadle

7. FORSBROOK

11. MILL MEECE

Uttoxeter

Eccleshall

Stafford

Burton

4. HEYWOOD

9. ORGREAVE

12. WYCHNOR BRID

14. CANNOCK   Lichfield

Wolverhampton

3. SEDGELEY

5. BIRMINGHAM

1.	**John Brough**	Murder	1845
2.	**Charles Brough**	Murder	1864
3.	**Richard Hale**	Infanticide	1864
4.	**Robert Lander**	Highway Robbery	1798
5.	**Edward Kidson**	Cattle Theft	1798
6.	**Stephen Barlow**	Riot	1783
7.	**Thomas James**	Bestiality	1811
8.	**Joseph Preston**	Incest	1828
9.	**Tommy Bond**	Murder	1895
10.	**George Ferns**	Forgery	1801
11.	**John Highfield**	Forgery	1828
12.	**Ann Statham**	Infanticide	1816
13.	**John Gold**	Murder	1811
14.	**'Nathaniel'**	Murder	1675

CONTENTS

One
A FAMILY AFFAIR
John Brough of Biddulph

By the time Thomas Brough had reached the age of forty eight, his status of small farmer had increased to that of a relatively prosperous landowner. This improvement to his fortune had been achieved by parsimonious habit and a cold, calculating approach to the accumulation of money.

His sister Judith referred to him as 'a selfish and unprincipled man, conducting himself with great cruelty towards his mother and relatives.' This also seemed to be the general opinion held by his neighbours and acquaintances.

Brough lived at High Bent Farm in the Parish of Biddulph, and had accumulated land and property thereabouts, including the adjoining farm of Whitefields. The two farmhouses were only 307 yards apart and connected by a footpath which crossed a rivulet some 128 yards from Whitefields.

Thomas's widowed mother and his brother John lived at Whitefields. Also living with them was the nine year old son of Thomas and John's sister, the old lady's grandson, who was also called John Brough.

Old Mrs Brough was the tenant of Whitefields, but John Brough managed the farm and paid the rent to his brother Thomas. By the beginning of January 1845, the rent was well in arrears and the acquisitive Thomas had run out of patience.

On January 3rd 1845, the bailiffs arrived, on instructions from Thomas, to try to collect the twenty nine pounds and twelve shillings owing. Having a visit from the bailiffs was shame enough, but to have one son send them against another...! Old Mrs Brough was understandably distraught and pleaded with someone to make the short journey between the two farms to fetch Thomas so that all could be resolved. Being sympathetic, the bailiffs sent for Thomas to try and arrange an amicable settlement.

One of the bailiffs, Thomas Mitchell, constable of the Parish of Biddulph, said of Thomas Brough; *'Thomas was rather rough and angry when put up; he was not a fighting man, but I think he was a hot-headed man. The family seemed to be afraid of him as a person who had power over them.'*

When Thomas arrived, adamant that the rent arrears should be paid, his mother fell to her knees in tears, pleading that they needed time to pay, and that they would be able to give him some of the money if he would just wait until they had sent a pig to market. The constable commented, *'Thomas passed her by and said nothing ...'*

On Thomas Brough's instructions, two boxes were removed by the bailiffs and taken to High Bent Farm. One contained some of John Brough's possessions, and the other some things belonging to another brother, James, a farm labourer living-in at Blackwood Hill Farm, then owned by Mr Challinor. It was obvious that Thomas intended to "sell them up" to recoup his rent.

As he was about to leave, John said to his brother, *'Stop a bit. I will go and kin' (*kindle*) my lanthorn and I will go with you as far as the barn and sweep two or three oats up...'*

The barn stood in the meadow between the two houses, on the left hand side going towards High Bent and some eighty yards from Whitefields.

According to little John Brough's account, his Uncle John came into the house, lit the candle in the lantern and went off in the direction of the barn. Uncle Thomas set off, crossing the meadow in the direction of High Bent. It was about six o'clock on a dark January evening.

Hannah Brough was Thomas's wife. They had no children of their own, but her nephew John Shufflebotham, a young lad of about sixteen years old, lived with them. On that fateful Friday Hannah had been to Tunstall to sell butter, and returned home just as it began to get dark. She asked her nephew of her husband's whereabouts and he told her that Thomas had just gone across to Whitefields.

Hannah knew about the unpaid rent, and that Thomas had been talking of fetching the bailiffs and assumed that he had "gone to be his own bailiff" and collect what was owing. She set about preparing supper as normal. By six o'clock however, when Thomas had not returned home, she asked her nephew to fetch a neighbour, Ishmael Lancaster, to help search for her errant husband.

As it happened, John decided to search on his own, and went out into the night, not a little scared, for who knows what might be abroad on Biddulph Moor in the dark? John recounts what happened next:-

'I went out of the house about six o'clock to listen if I could hear anything of my Uncle. It was towards the Whitefields I went. I had gone about half way. After I had waited about twenty minutes I heard a little groan and then something that

dragged upon the ground. I heard a rustle in the hedge. I then went home and felt desperate frightened. It was very dark. I did not see anything. I should think the place from which the noise appeared to come was about twenty yards from where I was. I heard some boys passing at the time. I could not see who they were, but I heard them say, "There's a boggot in the bush...!". I went home but did not tell my Aunt.'

It is easy to imagine young John standing nervously in the pitch darkness, straining his ears for the sound of his Uncle's return, and hearing instead a ghostly moan. Perhaps if he had been brave enough to investigate, he might have saved his Uncle's life.

Nine o'clock arrived and Thomas had still not come home. John Shufflebotham decided to fetch another neighbour, Thomas Pierpoint, to accompany him to Whitefields and when he arrived he saw only old Mrs Brough and her grandson. They were surprised and perturbed to hear that Thomas had not been seen at High Bent since five o'clock. She told John that he had left them at six and that his brother had followed.

Hannah and her nephew made several enquiries in the neighbourhood and went to the Talbot Inn, but nothing had been seen of Thomas. She was still out searching at three in the morning, accompanied now by a man named Bailey, and they returned to Whitefields yet again where they discovered that the elder John Brough had returned and was sitting by the fire. Old Mrs Brough heard the noise and shouted downstairs from her bed to ask what was amiss. Mr. Bailey shouted up to tell her that Thomas had not come home, and they were still out searching for him. Hannah said she feared that he *'had been made away...'*

Old Mrs Brough rose at seven the next morning and found John still sitting on the stool in front of the fire. She had heard him go outside for coal once or twice during the night and what with that and Hannah's visit, she had spent a very disturbed night. She asked him why he had not gone to bed and he replied that he had sat up late, then after Bailey and Hannah had come he had thought it was not worthwhile going to bed. John Brough was an extremely worried man!

At this point, confusingly, a second John Shufflebotham enters the story. He also lived at Biddulph and was a labourer, working for his father.

On Saturday January 4th, he had been to Woodhouse Green with his friend, William Stanier. On the way home the two separated, William going off to visit Stephen Lancaster and his wife, and John going home. As he passed Gledelow sand pit he glanced down into the pit and was shocked to see the body of a man. He ran after his departed friend and fetched him back and, accompanied by Stephen Lancaster's wife and one William Knight they clambered down into the pit to examine the macabre find, before rushing to the Talbot Inn to report their discovery. A party of searchers, including both young John Shufflebotham and John Brough hastened to the pit and gazed at their relative sprawled in the bottom. The search for Thomas Brough was over. John Brough was arrested on suspicion of murder shortly after, together with his brother James.

At the inquest, John Harrison, surgeon, of Burslem gave his clinical report:-

'We first examined the external parts of the head. On the left side there was an extensive contused wound, and on the right side, another. As we removed the scalp from the head and laid the wounded parts bare, the head on the left side was much fractured, and several pieces of bone had been removed which left the external covering of the brain completely bare. The injury and the fracture now spoken of were sufficient to cause death, and that death must have been instantaneous.'

He concluded that the injury on the right side was caused by a single blow, as was the one at the back, but those on the left must have been caused by several blows, the injuries being caused by a blunt instrument like a hammer.

After the body had been discovered a search had been made in the surrounding area for the murder weapon, and on the Saturday evening just such a likely weapon was found by Job Bailey, a stonemason living in the Parish of Horton. At the inquest he said,

'On Saturday evening I found the hammer, now produced, in a meadow which is part of Whitefield Farm and in the occupation of John Brough. It was about sixty yards from a spot where there was a quantity of blood. When I found the hammer it was wet, and there was blood on it with black hairs, the blood on the ground was on a steep bank at the bottom of which there was a little stream of water and it was in a direct line from the Whitefield Farm and the house of the deceased. The turf on the bank had been recently turned up as if to hide the blood. The stream of water appeared as if it had been dammed up. There was blood about the place. There was also blood in another hole.'

In his defence John Brough explained that the banks of the stream were always red, not with blood, but with 'carr' water, which came from some iron works upstream.

The hammer was identified as belonging to John Brough by both his distraught mother and by little John Brough. On that very Friday he had been using it to break stone and had left it reared up against a wall between the end of the house and the meadow gate. He had not seen it there the following morning.

As the case against John Brough began to mount, the most damning evidence came from his brother James, of Blackwood Hill Farm.

He had been feeding his master's horses between eight and nine in the evening on Friday January 3rd, when his brother John and his neighbour Ishmael Lancaster called to see him.

John had explained that their brother Thomas had taken

6

their boxes and was 'going to sell them up' and he wanted James to go with him right away.

James had been unperturbed and explained, *'It's so near the weekend, it's no use my going with thee tonight, he won't sell thee up this week.'*

John was eager that James go with him and sort it all out, but James was adamant that there was no rush and stayed to clean out the horses and check the cattle. After a hasty meal of bread and cheese they set off for Whitefields. Ishmael Lancaster stopped off at his own house, leaving the two Broughs to continue alone.

John insisted that James should call at High Bent to ask why his box was there. James agreed and called to see Hannah whilst John continued on his way back to Whitefields. Hannah of course knew little of what had transpired that day as she had been at Tunstall and could only tell him that Thomas had not returned. James muttered that *'It was a strange thing they could not be quiet.'* and that he was going to his mother's and would call again on his way back. He went off after John and soon caught up with him.

'Is he in?' inquired John.

James said that he had not been home since he had called at Whitefields.

At this John began to cry, sobbing that he did not know what he must do and that he reckoned he should hang.

James, rather confused, asked him 'What for?'

John confessed that he had hit Thomas on the back of the head with a hammer and he reckoned he had killed him, that the body was at the bottom of the meadow, and that James must help to do something with him, but James could only reply 'Oh dear John, I cannot go near him!'

John begged repeatedly, but James doggedly refused. Stunned at his brother's grisly revelation, James continued with the overwrought John to their mother's house. While James was

7

there, John again begged his help, but James was adamant that he could not go near Thomas.

James eventually left, leaving John in tears of desperation. On his way back to Blackwood Hill Farm he met Hannah and Ishmael Lancaster out searching and they asked him if he had seen Thomas. He replied 'No', which was true enough, and Hannah said that she *'doubted but that he was made away as he had never been home.'*

When John was arrested so too was James, but he was soon released.

At about six o'clock on the morning of the sixth of January 1845, the Monday following the murder, John Brough made a desperate bid for freedom. He and another person, in custody for stealing fowls, were being held at the Talbot Inn in Biddulph. They were in the charge of the parish constable, by whom they had been handcuffed together, but they found a stone, broke off the handcuffs and ran off in different directions.

John Brough only had a day of freedom however, as he was found at about noon on Tuesday concealed under some hay and straw in a hayloft. He said that when he escaped he had intended to kill himself, but had thought better of it and was intending to give himself up.

At his trial there was some mention of the fact that he may have been suddenly provoked by his brother, but the judge told the jury that if that were the case they must ask themselves, would there have been a blow at the back of the head ?

The jury found him guilty, with a recommendation for mercy because of his previous good character, but the judge sentenced him to death. Whilst he was in prison, Brough made the following statement:

'Thomas shortly after left. I followed him and kept begging and entreating him to let me have the boxes back again. I promised he should have the rent. He said he would not let me have them again that night but he would consider of it in

8

the morning, or by tomorrow at noon.

A little hammer for breaking stones was reared up against the stone wall in the yard aside of the gate which opens into the meadow. As I went along, I took it up and held it in my hand while talking to him. We stood a little bit, then we walked side by side talking to each other.

I kept on asking for the boxes back again, and said he should have his rent if he would only let the matter drop. He still refused. His selling us up and getting papers printed about the sale of the stock and things on the farm and his taking away the boxes aggravated me.

I then struck him on the head one blow, whether on the back or on the side I'm not sure. I don't know whether he had his back or his face turned towards me at that time. He stood a little bit after I had hit him and then fell down. I do not remember if he spoke after the blow was given. I took the hammer part of the way up the meadow and then flung it away. I then went straight home. I lighted a candle and went to the barn with it. I swept up some oats and shut the barn door.

I went to the cowhouse and looked at the cows and calves. I then went into the house and sat by the fire. My mother and the little boy were there. I remained but a few minutes and then got up and walked to the meadow to see whether my brother Thomas was gotten up and gone home. He was sitting up. I stood looking at Thomas and I perceived a person at the contrary side.' (This was the boy John Shufflebotham, searching for his uncle.)

'Thomas was in a bit of a hollow. The person I saw stood on the top of a bank. He was looking straight forward in the direction where Thomas was. I was frightened lest he should see me and stooped down by a ditch a little distance off from Thomas. The person was about twenty or thirty yards off. I was about five or six yards off from Thomas. Thomas was sitting on a place that sloped down to the ditch, and I afterwards heard a

9

splash in the water from Thomas's falling in. It is possible for a man to slip down into the water even if he has not been hurt.

At this moment the person who had been looking towards the place where my brother was moved on. I heard his step and thought he was coming where Thomas was. If he had come to his help I think Thomas would have lived. I was afraid to go myself and went off home immediately as fast as I could and washed myself.'

John Brough then recounts his going to fetch James, his confession and James's refusal to help, and then continues,

'I sat by the fireside all that night. I went out about five or six next morning, before Mother came downstairs. I returned to the meadow to the place where I had left Thomas the night before. I found his head and arms and half his body in the water. His feet were upon the bank. I pulled his body out of the ditch by the feet. I carried it in my arms several yards and then lifted it in a barrow which was close to our house. I wheeled it a little distance and then carried it again a considerable way and put it on the edge of a pit and let it roll down to the place where it was found. I then returned towards home. On my way back I wheeled away the barrow which was left behind when I took the body to the edge of the pit. I declare most solemnly , I did not intend to kill my brother or even to strike him, ten minutes before I did so.'

It seems that John Brough, who was *'tall, and of an unintelligent expression of countenance'* was of a quiet and mild disposition, and, in contrast to his brother Thomas, kind to his mother. Uneducated, he could read only slightly. At the time of his trial rumours began to circulate of an incestuous relationship with his sister, These were quickly squashed and refuted in a report in the Staffordshire Advertiser of April 5th 1845.

An attempt was made to have the sentence reduced to 'Transportation for Life' but John Brough was in mortal fear of the dreaded transportation, and said that he preferred to hang. He was given no option and the appeal was dismissed.

Excepting his immediate neighbours, the case did not excite much attention and only six hundred people were present at the execution. Understandably, John Brough spent a disturbed and sleepless night, and upon reaching the steps leading to the drop, he trembled so much that two prison officers had to help him to ascend.

Head bowed and weeping bitterly, his handkerchief to his face, his last words were *'I hope the Lord will have mercy on my poor soul.'*

There does seem to be a little mystery to the case. The doctor's evidence said that death had been instantaneous from several hammer blows - yet John Brough maintained that he had hit his brother only once, and that, when he went back later, Thomas was sitting up. That Thomas was alive at this time was corroborated to some extent by John Shufflebotham who had heard a moan and a dragging sound.

Did someone finish off the job which John had already started? Or was John trying to paint himself a little whiter? Was John Shufflebotham listening to the actual murder? We shall never know.

A visit to High Bent now reveals a vastly different house from the one occupied by Thomas and Hannah. The original four roomed cottage has been expanded by a succession of owners into a sizeable gentleman's residence, and when I visited was owned by an airline pilot, Mr Dave Waddington, and his family. The name of the farm has been changed over the years and the property has been variously known as the New House, High Bent Farm and Brough's Farm, but this association with the unfortunate family was obviously too much for someone, and it is now known simply as High

Bent.

When I visited Whitefields, it was occupied by Eliot Lancaster and presented a dark and towering aspect, and must have changed very little from the house occupied by John Brough and his mother. Walking across the fields which separate the two properties and crossing the little stream where the murder occurred, it is possible to stir the mud in the bottom of the ditch and see the iron deposits mentioned by John Brough, which stained the bank and water. Perhaps it was fanciful on Job Bailey's part to claim that it was Thomas's blood. Livestock treading through the stream would have caused the effects which Job described.

The deeds to High Bent reveal that with Thomas's death Hannah's problems were far from over. Thomas had made a will in 1830 naming Hannah as beneficiary, but as he had purchased property since that date and had not made another will, then as the law stood his heir at law was his brother John, the very man who had killed him! Since John had been executed for the murder, the property passed to Her Majesty, Queen Victoria.

On March 20th 1847 an Inquisition was held at the Swan Hotel, Stafford. The findings of the inquisition were that the property had legally passed to John Brough, that it had then become forfeit to the Crown, and that when he died Thomas Brough had been indebted to several people 'upon mortgage and simple contract', amounting to £650.

The Commission recommended to the Queen that, considering the circumstances the property should be granted to Thomas Redfern of Leek to sell. The debts, plus expenses, totalled £696.15s.3d. and Hannah managed to raise this and reclaim the property. In 1859 she married one Clement Bailey, carefully recording that her property remained *free from the control debts or engagements of Clement Bailey or any future*

12

husband or husbands.'

Following her death in March 1868, the property eventually passed to James Shufflebottom who sold it to John Shufflebottom, an earthenware dealer of St. Helens, Lancs for £900. In 1880 he used it to raise one hundred pounds, mortgaging the property to a Michael McGhee of St. Helens. In 1881, John Shufflebottom died and the property was inherited by his daughter, Mary Bates.

In April 1896, an order was made by the court of Chancery of the County Palatine of Lancaster, Liverpool district, in favour of Michael McGhee, the plaintiff in the case of McGhee v Bates, who was claiming his one hundred pounds plus interest.

It was ordered that the amount should be charged against the property, which was to be sold and the money paid to the court, *'in payment of what should be certified to be due to the plaintiff for principal interest and costs.'*

Ironically, in the end it was the owners of High Bent Farm who were 'sold up', and not the occupants of Whitefields.

Tower at the North West Angle of Gaol at Stafford 1843   S.Richards

Two
THE FALLEN TENANT
Charles Brough of Audley

On 26th December 1864, nineteen years after the execution of John Brough, his nephew Charles Brough suffered the same fate and it was for a very similar type of murder. Beginning in 1840, a series of murders had been committed in the Audley area. Charles Brough was found guilty of the fourth of these murders.

The series started with the killing of the Parish Constable, named Beech, in the grounds of Apedale Hall, the work of poachers. Then William Cooper, a gamekeeper's son, was shot by a discontented poacher on the threshold of his father's house, The Hays, at Halmerend. Next, an old man hawking small wares at Alsager's Bank had been brutally murdered, his head severed and burnt on the fire of his murderer's cottage. The fourth murder was in 1864 when

15

Charles Brough killed a seventy five year old man named George Walker.

George Walker was a man fallen on hard times. At the age of thirty he had taken on the tenancy of Bignall Hill Farm, near Audley, a fairly substantial holding of some hundred and twenty acres, which he farmed successfully for some twenty years.

When it came to lending money George was a soft touch, and he was eventually owed so much by friends and neighbours that he fell into financial difficulties. When his business foundered he was forced to relinquish the tenancy of Bignall Hill Farm.

Then for many years George worked as a labourer, but despite being a steady, intelligent and hard working man, he never managed to raise himself to his previous comfortable level.

Still very much attached to the farm which he had worked so lovingly for twenty years, in 1861 he had received permission from the tenant, Mr Barrows, to occupy an old 'drumble'*.

The half acre piece of waste land lay about a quarter of a mile from Bignall Hill Farmhouse, and George set about reclaiming and cultivating the patch of ground. He also constructed a little hut for himself, which was only six feet by five feet by four feet high. It was made out of stones and boards, with a roof of turf and rubbish. The floor was bare earth and the door consisted of a few rotten boards. Inside were the barest of necessities. His sleeping 'couch' consisted of boards covered in hay.

On Lady Day 1864, Mr W Rhodes took over the tenancy of Bignall Hill Farm and gave old George Walker notice to quit his drumble hole at the end of the summer. George made arrangements to move in with relatives, but intended to stay on his little plot until the last possible moment, the end of

*A small quarry or working, often a marl pit.

the agricultural tenancy at Michaelmas.

On Wednesday July 27th 1864 George strolled into Audley village. He went down Ravens Lane to visit his brother-in-law, Ralph Warburton and asked Ralph to lend him sixpence to tide him over until Monday, when he intended to go into Newcastle to collect some rent due to him for a piece of land he owned. Ralph gave him half a crown and a little later George went back to his hut.

On that same evening he was visited by his good friend John Norcop, who often called round to see the old man, and on this occasion they had spent some considerable time discussing the 'Mr Briggs Railway Carriage Murder' - a notorious London case. George had not seen a newspaper that day and was interested to hear of the latest developments. John Norcop left at seven o'clock, promising to return the following evening, Thursday.

When he returned as arranged he was horrified to see his old friend's body, dressed only in a ragged shirt, lying outside his hut. He was about three feet from the door on his right hand side with his hands under his face.

John Norcop knew something was amiss, but was too frightened to go nearer to the body to investigate and so he ran off to fetch some neighbours.

Upon closer investigation it quickly became obvious that Old George had been brutally beaten about the head and face. His little hut had been broken into by the simple expedient of pulling out a small section of the wall by the door and then reaching in to unlatch it from the inside. The police were called and P.C. White and P.C. Earp arrived at the hut. Upon entering they were confronted by a scene of utter chaos. The walls were blood spattered and it seemed that George had been murderously attacked whilst lying on his makeshift bed. He had been robbed of the half crown given to him by Ralph, and of a watch which George had exchanged with John Norcop for another.

John Norcop had bought the watch five months previously and was able to describe it with great accuracy. Of thick German silver, it carried the identification number 45177, and sported a plain dial with Roman figures. It also had a thick brass chain with a small seal and key.

James Obery of Wood Lane, an under-gamekeeper, stated that *'only a week before the murder I watched George carve the numbers of the watch upon his door frame with a distinctive knife with a broken tip.'* This statement proved conclusively that the watch had been in George's possession until only a week before his death.

On Friday afternoon, July 29th, James David Jones was working as a pawnbroker's assistant in the Tunstall shop of his employer, Mr Hulme. A man entered the shop asking twenty five shillings for a watch.

The young man was alert, and suspecting that it was the one which had been stolen from the murdered man at Audley, he left the customer in the shop under some pretext, and went off to get the police. He returned with Sgt. Harrison and P.C. Cooke, who asked the customer where he had obtained the watch. He replied that he had obtained it three weeks previously from one William Smith of Crackley, and he gave his name as Charles Jones of Red Street. The police took him into custody. Blood was found on his clothing, and a knife with a broken tip was discovered in his pocket, together with two half crowns, one shilling, one sixpence and one penny. He was then charged with the murder of George Walker. He said nothing except that the goods belonged to his parents and his name was Charles Brough.

At seven o'clock on Friday evening, Charles asked P.C. Woolley for some water, and when the constable took it through into the cells for him Brough said;

'I took the watch from Mr Walker. Is he dead?'

'I believe he is.' replied P.C. Woolley.

'Poor fellow, I did not go with the intention to kill him. I have had no work since April. I have been troubled with diabetes. My father and I had some words about me not being able to work and I started to go from home. I went to the old man's hut thinking of going to sleep. He must have heard me for he came to the door. There was a piece of wood lying near the door - a wheel spoke from an ox-cart. I picked it up and struck his head with it. I could not see whether it hit the old man or not, but he shouted so I struck him again. I then struck a match and took the watch out of his pocket and walked off'

Inspector Scott then went to Brough's cell and cautioned him.

'I did it.' Brough replied. *'There was no-one with me. I was alone.'*

The inquest was held at the Plough Inn, Ravens Lane. The evidence given by the surgeon who had conducted the post-mortem was not compatible with Brough's claim that he had only hit George twice. Neither was Brough's statement compatible with the evidence of the blood on the walls and the place where the body was found.

Richard Vernon conducted the post mortem on Friday evening. He found coagulated blood between the bone and the skin over the left ear and extensive fractures, with the front part of the head and nasal bones also fractured. Injuries which had been inflicted by a heavy boot or clog. The fractures had been the cause of death.

The coroner stated that George Walker's head must have been hit with a blunt instrument (the wooden spoke) and a sharp iron bar some fifty or sixty times. Both weapons came from the shack.

At Brough's trial the defence tried to get the case reduced to a charge of manslaughter on the grounds that diabetes was both mentally and physically debilitating, but the judge maintained that diabetes did not stop a man from knowing right from wrong, so the charge must be murder or nothing. The jury found him guilty.

Charles Brough bore little resemblance to his Uncle John. He was described as '*... a man below middle height with sandy hair and no whiskers, suffering from an internal complaint, and could scarcely walk alone...*' He was quite indifferent to everything that was taking place around him.

He was hanged on December 26th 1864. Over a hundred police were brought into Stafford, for a large crowd was expected. Not only was it a bank holiday, but a market was being held in Stafford on the same day.

In the event, according to a report in the Staffordshire Advertiser, only between six and eight thousand people assembled. The reporter commented that the onlookers were of mixed character, many of them well dressed, but the majority were colliers, many of them with unwashed faces' *.... the features of many of both sexes were repulsive and suggested the vast field of missionary work which lies close to our own door.....*'

Three
IN THE CORN FIELD
Richard Hale of Sedgeley

Charles Brough did not die alone, for his was a double hanging. On the gallows with him was Richard Hale of Sedgeley, convicted of the murder of his daughter, Eliza Silleto, aged six.

Richard Hale looked older than his thirty years. Short, broad and powerful, Hale must have been a brute of a man, considering the treatment he meted out to Eliza and her mother.

The daughter of Hale and Mary Silleto, Eliza had been born out of wedlock. When she was four years old, her mother died of starvation, for which Richard Hale served a term of imprisonment. Left to the tender mercies of her father, Eliza soon became a nuisance and Hale had frequently been heard to claim that he would 'get rid of her.'

The little girl lived with Hale and his mother and at four o'clock on the afternoon of Wednesday, July 20th 1864, her

21

grandmother reported her missing.

At two o'clock the child had gone off in the direction of Bilston, complaining that she had *'been beaten for nothing at all.'* Hale had tied on the child's bonnet before she left, and when she was later reported missing, he joined in the search.

Following the death of his wife, Richard Hale had taken up with a tall, sharp-featured woman of thirty called Cecilia Baker. Her sister Hannah Baker saw Eliza at about a quarter past two on that fatal July day. The little girl was crying, clutching a crust of bread. When Hannah asked where she was going, little Eliza only sobbed *'I'm going and I'm not coming back'* and set off in the direction of Daisy Bank which was near Coseley Church.

Some little time after two o'clock, John Jones, a hairdresser from Coseley, was in a field near Coseley Church, when he noticed Cecilia Baker, whom he had known for six or seven years, with Richard Hale whom he also knew slightly. The couple were walking with Eliza along the hedgeside of a wheatfield, towards the railway. They stopped opposite a gravel hole, as if they were selecting a place to sit. Hale took the little girl down the hole and seemed to make a suggestion to Cecilia Baker, but she appeared to disagree with him.

All three moved along the hedgeside, turned left and walked deliberately into the wheat. Hale trampled some corn flat around Eliza and Cecilia and the two adults sat down in the clearing. Cecilia threw the child to Hale and then got up and looked towards Jones. The little girl ran off into the corn. Hale ran after her, caught her and brought her back, threw her onto the floor and knelt beside her. He drew his handkerchief from his pocket, and Jones thought the child was perhaps bruised or grazed and that Hale was going to bandage the wound. Eliza shrieked and then her cries began to get fainter. To Jones she appeared to be crying herself to sleep.

John Jones had noted all this as he was walking along,

and eventually the three disappeared from view. When the field came into view again, he could see none of them.

Two other people claimed to have seen Eliza that day. Esther Richards, Hale's sister, lived next door but one to Hale and his mother, and she said that she had seen Eliza at approximately two o'clock. The school bell had been ringing when Eliza had spoken to her. The child had then gone off to the school, which lay opposite the cornfield. Esther also maintained that Hale was kind to the child and utterly refuted the rumour which began to fly soon after Eliza's disappearance - that on the afternoon in question her brother had brought home a knife and had washed his hands. Esther insisted that she had not seen her brother that day after dinner time.

At half past four on July 20th, Mrs Ann Dudley said that she saw Hale threatening Eliza. She heard him say that he supposed she had been '*visiting Mrs Johnson's and she would never go there again - he'd give her enough to finish her !'*

Mrs Dudley remonstrated with him and said that if he misused the little girl again she would go to the police. She received a mouthful of obscenities for her trouble and only half an hour later heard that Eliza Silleto was missing. Eliza remained missing for a fortnight.

On Tuesday, August 2nd 1864, Edward Clarke, a boatbuilder, was walking with his dog beside the cornfield. After running about in and out of the corn, the dog ran up to Clarke and began tugging at his master's trouser leg, then running back into the corn. Curious at this odd behaviour he decided to follow his dog and found the body of a little girl in a much-trampled area of corn. The little body was on its back, with the clothes rucked up to the waist, and this subsequently gave rise to speculation that she had been sexually assaulted before her death.

The hot summer weather had reduced the body to such a state of decomposition that only the legs and arms remained entire. It was impossible to detect any wounds on the body, and there were no fractures, but from the bloodstained clothing and a bloodstained handkerchief found eight yards from the body, and the excessively trampled corn it was obvious that Eliza's end had been a violent one. Robert Tupman, a police sergeant from Coseley, was summoned to the body. Shortly afterward Hale came up and seeing the body, threw up his hands and cried 'Oh my child!' then turned and ran away.

Subsequent enquiries pointed a suspicious finger at Hale and Baker. Oddly, they had been seen by several people in the vicinity of the cornfield during the period that Eliza had been missing. Sergeant Tupman arrested Hale. When asked if he wanted to make a statement, he said that he was innocent and that he had not seen the child from the time he tied her bonnet until he saw her body.

On August 3rd, Police Sergeant McRea of Bilston apprehended Cecilia Baker, saying that she was accused of murdering the child with Richard Hale.

She said, *'Richard Hale met me here on the day the child was lost, and we walked home together. When we got home someone told me that the child had not come home, and that was the first time that I knew the child was missing.'* She added that she left work at six o'clock and that she supposed it was Hale's sister who had been saying things about her.

McRea then told her that it was being said that she had been seen in the wheatfield on Friday June 29th .

'Yes, but I was never off the walk. I loved the child too well to do anything to it,' she replied and also explained that she walked along that pathway by the wheatfield every day on her way to and from work. She was released through lack of evidence, but when the hairdresser, John Jones, eventually came forward, she was reapprehended on October 12th.

Jones had been very slow to make a statement and had not done anything until after the initial inquest. His reasons

24

were that he had heard that a child was missing and had been subsequently found murdered, but he did not know which child, and did not know that Hale and Baker lived together. Also, he disliked being a witness and having to travel to Stafford to give evidence. The inquest and trial produced some horrific tales of Richard Hale's treatment of his little daughter.

Sixty year old Mary Johnson of Legg Lane, Coseley, said that Richard Hale and his daughter had lodged with her from April 1863 until July 16th, 1864. She told the court that Hale had treated Eliza very badly, subjecting her to frequent beatings. On one occasion he had aimed a kick at the child but Mrs Johnson had rushed to Eliza's defence. She had pushed Hale down, shouting *'You shall not kill her here!'*

Hale replied, *'I have got to be hung and may as well be hung for that young b........ as another!'*

On another occasion when Mrs Johnson caught him beating Eliza, she had said to him *'I think your love's all gone away from this child.'* and he had replied *'Yes, it has, this month ago.'* He said he would leave the country if it wasn't for the child. After leaving his lodging with Mary Johnson, Hale went to stay with his mother in Yew Tree Lane.

Thomas Johnson, Mary's husband, recounted another incident. One night Hale had come home drunk, a not unusual occurrence, and the next morning Eliza had dropped the poker, aggravating his hangover. Hale had struck out at her, hitting her with his fist and knocking her against the oven. Again Mrs Johnson had spoken out against Hale's brutality.

'I've seen a picture of the gallows in bed and I may as well be hung for her as not.' he replied. He had also bragged to Mrs Johnson that he often abused the child when he was sober, as well as when drunk.

On Wednesday, July 27th, at two in the afternoon, Ann Westwood had passed Hale going down Yew Tree Lane with his mother. She said that she had heard Hale say to his mother,

'You d..... old b........, you have driven away the child and now you want to drive me!'

His mother had made a most peculiar reply. *'No Dick I didn't. You carried it off in a bag.'*

Several people deposed to having seen both Hale and Baker in the wheatfield on several occasions. Mary Diggory saw them both there on the Saturday after Eliza's disappearance. She had spoken to them but they had not answered.

On Friday July 29th, William Eldon, a shingler, saw them standing together in the wheatfield. He spoke to Hale who "dowked" (ducked) his head to avoid him and went into the road with Cecilia.

John Bough, a stocktaker, paused in his walk near the wheatfield at one o'clock on the same day when he saw a short man and a tall woman going between two fields of barley. He sat down on the railway embankment and lost sight of them. Shortly afterwards they came from the spot where the body was subsequently found. Originally he had said that he could not be sure that the two people were Hale and Baker, but later changed his mind and made a positive identification.

Also on July 29th, Lillian Elden saw Hale, who ducked down. She went on a little further and saw Cecilia Baker, some three or four yards into the wheat and about fifteen yards from Hale. When Hale got up Lillian Elden shouted *'How do you do, Dick lad?'*

He said nothing, but hid in the ditch. Next she had seen Hale and Baker leaving the field together. A little further along the track she had encountered John Bough.

However, there were others to testify that whoever the woman was, it was not Cecilia Baker. Elizabeth Round, wife of Joseph Round. Catherine Carrier wife of a miner living at Highfields and George Jones a boatbuilder. All were in the employ of Mr Philip Williams, who lived near to where the body was found and they swore positively that Cecilia went there to work in the morning as usual on the day in question and that she did not leave work or the sight of the witnesses for a single hour that day until she left work as usual in the evening.

The evidence given by Mr John Smith, the surgeon who had assisted J.M. Ballenden in the post mortem was particularly graphic. Those of an imaginative nature may prefer not to read the following details.

Mr John Smith said that he had been shown down a trodden track in the field which terminated in a furrow, and at the end there was a child. The track commenced from the side of the field next to a high and thick hedge and on that side of the hedge there was no proper path, hence the track could not be seen from the footpath except by stooping down and looking through the bottom of the hedge.

The body was lying on its back, the fingers and toes were clenched with the trunk higher than the head. Parts of the body had been eaten by rats, and had maggots and beetles in it. The clothes and the ground were covered with blood. It was impossible to tell if the throat had been cut as the neck was decomposed. If the blood over and around the body had been caused by a ruptured blood vessel, which can occur in some people when excited or under stress, then it is possible to bleed to death through the mouth, Excessive stomach pain could have caused the fingers to curl, but would not have caused the toes to curl. A ruptured blood vessel would also have meant that the fingers would have uncurled upon death. The surgeon stated plainly that he had only ever seen hands and feet in this state when caused by excessive violence or poison.

The legs and arms were the only parts of the body remaining entire. The head and limbs became dislodged when the body was moved. The boots were off and the socks were tucked inside them. The hat was a little distance from the body and the handkerchief which belonged to her father, and which she had been wearing pinned to the front of her dress like an apron, was lying eight yards away.

Dr. Wrightson, Professor of Chemistry at Sydenham College, Birmingham, had examined the handkerchief, clothes, soil and scalp and found all to be stained with human blood. He had found evidence of at least two ounces on the handkerchief, but as silk is not an especially absorbent material, much more would have passed through. Blood was also on the ribbons of the bonnet and the front of the dress. On the handkerchief was a one inch cut and in the same place, dried blood and light hair.

Dr. Wrightson had also examined Hale's clothing and found what appeared to be blood which had been partially removed by washing, but Dr. Wrightson would not swear to this. It is possible that the handkerchief was at such a considerable distance from the body having been dragged there by a rat, or it could have been pulled off as the little girl tried to escape from her attacker.

During the trial Hale appeared to be deaf and had to have everything repeated to him by a turnkey. Cecilia Baker, who was pregnant, was obviously in considerable discomfort throughout the whole proceedings.

The Defence argued that Hale had a hasty and violent temper which was inconsistent with the cool planning and execution of a murder which the Prosecution seemed to be implying, and that if the threats Hale had allegedly made really did portend murder, they would not have been uttered before witnesses, and must be taken as *'violent expressions of the unrestrained temper of an uneducated man.'*

The defence also claimed that the Prosecution's case, which alleged that Hale's motive for the murder was to get rid of the child, was not very substantial, since he could have been rid of her more easily by giving her to Mrs Johnson, whose obvious love for the child could have solved that particular problem.

The defence pointed out discrepancies in evidence given by witnesses. Jones had said that Hale and Baker were in the wheatfield at two o'clock but the child had been seen in the town as late as half past four. Hale's mother's odd remark was dismissed as just an idle comment as it was inconsistent with the Prosecutions' evidence. Also, the defence asked, why keep returning to the body - presumably to watch it decompose - when they could easily have buried the evidence? Jones's evidence was dismissed because of his delay in coming forward and the Defence claimed that the cause of death was bleeding to death naturally.

The Jury took fifty three minutes to convict both the accused. Cecilia Baker had to be carried from the court because of the pain she was suffering from her pregnancy. She was granted a stay of execution until the birth. The baby was born on February 19th 1865 and Cecilia Baker was granted a pardon.

No such clemency was extended to Hale. The night before his execution he continually expressed his innocence and never slept, passing the night either sitting on the bed or pacing the cell floor, reading the Bible or praying. He said to the warder who was with him, *'I have told the Sheriff I am innocent, and when I get the drop I shall tell the Chaplain the very same as I tell you now.'*

On the scaffold he said to the chaplain, *'Believe me sir, oh, believe me. Don't let the thought of my being guilty trouble you after I am gone, for sir, I am innocent.'*

Brough, who was to be executed alongside Hale, was more composed than his companion. Hale was obviously nervous and stumbled, showing signs of great trepidation. Both died quickly, though witnesses saw Hale's hands rise for a moment. The bodies were left to hang for an hour, then were taken down and placed in unmarked coffins and buried in the same grave near the chapel. Lime was flung on them to destroy them and thus *'preserve the prison from noxious gases and decomposing bodies.'*

  It seems unlikely, considering the nature of the man, that Hale was innocent as he claimed, but it is just feasible that another person took advantage of the opportunity presented by Eliza wandering around on her own to keep out of her father's way, to molest and brutally end her short unhappy life.

Four
GOD DAMN YOU AND THE GALLOWS TOO!
Robert Lander of Haywood

Suffering 'The Drop' for highway robbery has always had a
romantic bravado about it. The popular conception of the
handsome highwayman astride his mettlesome horse, bidding
the driver and passengers of the mail coach to 'Stand and
Deliver!' is actually a very far cry from the truth. The majority
of felons convicted of highway robbery were merely today's
weasel-like muggers dressed in period costume.

One such was Robert Lander, also known as Robert
Bradbury, born at Haywood near Stafford. He had a poor start
in life, bearing the unfortunate stigma of illegitimacy, which
was quite a drawback in the eighteenth century. Upon the death
of his father, however, Lander found himself in possession of a

few hundred pounds. At the age of twenty one he tried to gain employment in the excise department, but did not succeed and eventually found himself a job with some gentlemen engaged in the wine and spirit trade. He only stayed in their employment for a few months, during which he appears to have developed a fondness for their stock, as he was reported to spend a considerable amount of time in a state of intoxication.

At length he decided that he had had enough of the wine and spirit trade, no doubt after a series of warnings about tippling the stock, and he absconded, taking a watch belonging to one of his employers, which he sold in Stafford.

He enlisted in a regiment of foot, but finding that he liked that even less, he deserted and approached his former employers. Rather generously, considering his previous conduct, they agreed to purchase his discharge and he returned to his old job. Robert had money deposited with his employers, presumably from his father's legacy, and they handed over £120 which he managed to spend within a few weeks.

He subsequently took the King's Shilling no less than four times, by enlisting in four different regiments and immediately deserting from them all!

By March 1798 he had decided to try his hand at Highway Robbery, where, *'on the King's Highway, near Teddesley Park, he feloniously assaulted Solomon Bennet of Liverpool, wax chandler, and robbed him of one guinea and two half guineas in gold and thirty shillings and upwards in silver.'*

A fair haul in comparison with the King's Shilling which seemed to have been his previous source of income, but he paid for it with his life. He was caught and condemned in August 1798. As the judge concluded the sentence with *' and may the Lord have mercy on their souls.'*, Lander created an uproar in the court by leaping to his feet and shouting back at the Judge . *'God damn you and the gallows too, I care for neither'*!'

Five
HANGED FOR A SHEEP?
Edward Kidson of Birmingham

Condemned at the same Assizes was Edward Kidson, who was charged along with Richard Wilcox of stealing two cows, the property of a Birmingham butcher James Vize. Wilcox was acquitted, but Edward Kidson joined Robert Lander on the gallows.

Kidson had been given ample opportunity to be a law abiding citizen, but failed to learn his lessons. Six years previously at the Stafford Lent Assizes of 1792, he had been convicted of sheep stealing, for which he had been sentenced to hang, but was reprieved, the sentence being commuted to seven years transportation.

Whilst Kidson was on board the hulks his friends had managed to obtain a remission of the remainder of the sentence, but he could not resist the temptation of Mr. Vize's cows, and the law did not give him a second chance.

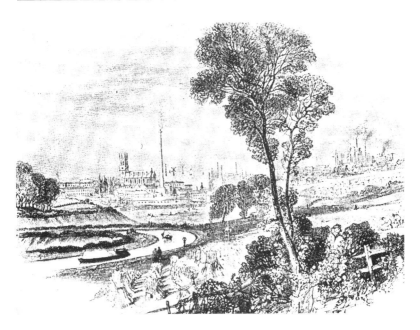

Six
THE POTTERS' BREAD RIOTS
Stephen Barlow of Etruria

Another Staffordshire resident who defied the law and paid with his life, was Stephen Barlow of Etruria. He was hanged for something which is now commonplace. Political demonstration and industrial unrest are routine occurrences in present times, but in 1783 inciting others to riot carried the death penalty.

For those not cushioned against life's hardships by gentle birth into a wealthy family, 1783 was a hard year. Food had been scarce for several years and inevitably it was the poor who suffered the most. Grinding poverty was widespread and bread had become so hard to obtain that the general dissatisfaction began to boil over into riots in many areas of the country.

The majority of the population were of the opinion that

the shortage of food was aggravated by traders who actually withheld foodstuffs in order to increase prices. In Etruria, Stoke on Trent, a full scale riot erupted.

The ringleaders were Stephen Barlow and Joseph Boulton, two Etruscan potters employed at Wedgwood's Etruria works. Stephen Barlow was the most vociferous and he was the one the authorities chose to make an example of, regardless of the fact that he had a wife and four small children.

Barlow had been born at Handley Green and at the time of the riot was thirty eight years of age. A broadsheet of 1783 claimed that he had been a soldier in the Staffordshire militia; *'..... out of which he was drummed for his bad behaviour; he has ever since practised an abandoned and indolent way of life and as an instance of it was one of the ring leaders in the late riots of Etruria and in the course of the disturbances was remarkably active...'*

How much of the substance of the broadsheet was an attempt by the authorities to discredit Barlow in an attempt to diffuse an explosive situation it is difficult to say. They needed his execution to be a lesson to other would-be rioters, and had no intention of turning him into a martyr who would be the focus of discontent. He had to be seen as an evil influence leading the good people of the Potteries astray.

The Etruria riot was triggered by the arrival of a canal boat laden with flour, which was tied to the wharf on the opposite side to the Wedgwood factory. The cargo was intended for provisions dealers in the pottery towns, and the arrival of the barge had been greeted with joy and enthusiasm by the hungry populace who saw a temporary alleviation of their misery.

However, the owners of the barge and its contents had learned that a fatter profit was to be made by by-passing the Potteries altogether, and selling the flour in Manchester. When it became general knowledge that the barge was to continue up the canal to Manchester the jubilant mood of the crowd turned to fury. As word spread a huge crowd, composed mainly of people from Etruria, began to assemble.

This mob was headed by Barlow and Boulton. The barge had by this time started its extended journey to Manchester, but the crowd ran after it. The barge was overtaken at Longport and hauled back to Etruria, where it was found to contain not only flour but cheese as well, a regular feast for the starving Etruscans. It is to their credit that, despite being so hard pressed, there was no looting.

It is a tribute to Barlow's leadership that he kept the mob in order and organised the unloading of the provisions. He sold them to the crowd at a reduced price and then handed over the proceeds to the captain of the barge, to be given to the owners. By this time a second barge drew up and this was similarly treated.

Had this been the only incident, things may have been smoothed over, but at this point the situation began to get out of hand. A few of the rioters stole a large quantity of staves from the crate shop in the Wedgwood factory. When they returned for more they encountered resistance and retaliated by setting fire to the building. A man named Lowndes attempted to stop them but the mob repaid him for his trouble by rushing off and setting fire to his house.

The mob were still in possession of the barges and they held them all that night. It was Friday and wild celebrations continued throughout the night with bonfires lit in the fields alongside the canal.

On Saturday, the mob was swelled by the arrival of many people from the surrounding districts. During the night the militia were called in, and under cover of darkness were able to get into the Etruria Inn. Major Sneyd was in command and had a detachment of the Staffordshire militia and a company of the Welsh Fusiliers who were stationed at Newcastle. When their arrival was discovered the infuriated crowd gathered in front of the Etruria Inn, from the windows of which Major Sneyd and two magistrates appealed to the crowd for order.

Things quietened down on the Sunday and as most people went home it began to seem that the whole thing might fizzle out, but on Monday the crowds, headed by Barlow and Boulton, returned in even greater numbers. This time the Riot Act was read in the presence of two magistrates.

The crowd was volatile and potentially violent. Major Sneyd and his men were patient and restrained despite the fact that many of the rioters now became very daring and insulting, particularly Barlow and Boulton. As one of the magistrates appealed to the crowd for calm, Barlow is reputed to have shouted, ' - *that he might order the soldiers to fire as soon as he pleased, for that he did not care for anything that might ensue from either him or any assistance he could get !*'

An hour passed and it became increasingly obvious that a very ugly scene was about to ensue and that the militia were going to be compelled to enforce order. Before the order to charge was issued, the magistrates made one final appeal. Whilst so doing one of them had a very narrow escape from a musket ball, fired accidentally. Nerves were strung to breaking point and the musket ball whistled past the magistrate and lodged in the lintel of the door of the Etruria Inn, the mark being pointed out as a curiosity to visitors for many years afterwards.

With no alternative left, Major Sneyd eventually gave the order to charge. Confronted with a disciplined band of soldiers the rioters broke and fled, the whole area erupting in confusion as people sped hither and thither in an effort to escape. The majority fled over the Etruria Hall fields and along the country lane which later formed the Etruria Grove.

Several of the officers and men recognised Barlow from the time he had spent in the militia, so after the dispersal of the crowd he was tracked down to his home with little difficulty. On the following night the Peace Officer arrived to arrest him. Barlow endeavoured to escape by climbing up the chimney, but in his efforts and haste he dislodged some bricks, drawing attention to himself.

When a search was made, he was found naked, huddled on the roof. The Peace Officer asked him to go along quietly, but defiantly he shouted that *'neither they nor a stronger force should oblige him to comply!'* and immediately endeavoured to make his escape *' by using every effort in his power for the destruction of his antagonists'*, presumably by throwing whatever bricks and missiles on which he could lay hands. Even when eventually captured, he refused to dress himself and was taken naked, despite the cold and the distance, from Etruria to Newcastle.

All these events and Barlow's dogged defiance hardened the attitude of the authorities to the disturbances and both Barlow and Boulton faced the capital charge. Boulton was reprieved but Barlow was condemned and hanged at Sandyford, Stafford, on Monday 17th March 1783 *'... for assembling in a riotous manner with other persons and committing divers outrages at Etruria in the County of Stafford...'*

He was accompanied to the gallows by the under-sheriff, gaoler, bailiffs and no less than three companies of the Staffordshire militia. The authorities were taking no chances of a possible rescue attempt or a repeat performance by the Etruscan rioters. Barlow's body was taken away by his supporters and family and buried in Stoke Churchyard.

The riots had seriously shaken the complacency of the authorities. It was generally felt that Barlow had been used as an example, and Josiah Wedgwood was sufficiently rattled to write a pamphlet addressed to his work people exhorting them to better conduct in the future. The writer of a broadsheet circulating after the execution deplores the committing of acts of violence and disturbing the County *'... because the Almighty has withheld his Blessing of plenty..'* and admonishes people to look back and compare how much worse were former times. *'... we may now hope for a plentiful year and the advantages of peace along with it, but if we should be denied the comfort of plenty will our impatient murmurings and disorderly assembling mend the matter? Certainly not. It will only aggravate our present distress, if it may be called so...'* .

When compared with present day penalties for such offences, Barlow's sentence was extreme. Punishments were far more severe prior to the twentieth century. The court placed greater emphasis on the record of the accused and persistent offenders could expect increasingly punitive sentences.

Seven
A BESTIAL ACT
Thomas James of Forsbrook

One capital conviction, however, cannot be explained away like that of Stephen Barlow. It concerns one Thomas James, a first offender from Forsbrook near Stoke-on-Trent, who was executed for bestiality, a comparatively minor offence when viewed from our more permissive times. He was convicted on the evidence of just one man, and it is unfortunate that no court records survive of the trial to enable Thomas James to defend himself to posterity. Only the deposition of the sole witness, Thomas Inskip, lies dustily in the Public Record Office in Chancery Lane.

Because of the sexual nature of the offence, very little appears in the newspapers of the time. All kinds of horrific

41

details of murders were recorded meticulously, but Georgian society was so scandalised by the nature of such cases that it was reported only in the most guarded of terms.

At Stafford Assizes in September 1811 Thomas James was charged that:

'..not having the fear of God before his eyes, nor regarding the order of nature but being moved and seduced by the instigation of the devil on the twelfth day of April with force and arms with a certain female ass then and there being feloniously wickedly, diabolically and against the order of nature had a certain venereal and carnal intercourse and then and there feloniously wickedly diabolically and against the order of nature carnally knew the said female ass and then and there feloniously wickedly diabolically and against the order of nature did permit and perpetrate that detestable and abominable crime of buggery (not to be named amongst Christians) to the great displeasure of Almighty God and to the great scandal of all human kind against the form of the statute in such case made and provided and against the peace of our Lord the King his Crown and dignity.'

Thomas James was just an ordinary village man. A sixty year old labourer with a wife and family, he must have been utterly bewildered by the turn that events were taking.

The start of his downfall began on May 12th 1811 when Thomas Inskip made a deposition before the Reverend E. Powys. He claimed that around four o'clock on the afternoon of Good Friday he saw Thomas James following a she-ass going into a field near the Stone House in Dilhorne.

Thomas Inskip went on to say that he was approaching from a field away from Thomas James and when he was within ten or twelve yards he saw him:

'......standing up to the back part of the she-ass and that his yard was in the privy part of the she-ass, that he perceived the she-ass move forward and his yard came out.'

He then claims that he:

'......*saw Thomas James take hold of his yard and put it into the she-ass again.*'

Thomas Inskip maintained that he spoke to Thomas James and made himself known, but that Thomas James went off without speaking. Inskip says that he then went up to the donkey ' *and saw her privy parts were wet.*'

Inskip was obviously illiterate. He signed his deposition with a scratchy, heavy-handed X against his name, but he had not yet finished damning Thomas James, choosing to add further details to the deposition. He went on to claim that Thomas James had followed the donkey up and down the field for between ten minutes and a quarter of an hour and that:

'*... when Thomas James took his yard out of the ass I saw something resembling a man's or an asses' seed lying upon the ground behind the ass. Also that the seed hung down the privy parts of the ass as she held her tail out...*'.

Reading between the lines of the deposition, it seems that Rev Powys knew the seriousness of the charge which was likely to arise from Inskip's accusations and was trying to provide another explanation - that the donkey was wet because she was in season, for it is then recorded that there were some jack asses in the adjoining field and that Thomas Inskip had seen one of them serving the female as he had walked to work that morning. Inskip again made his mark against this addition to his statement.

Four days later, on May 16th, Inskip adds even more to the deposition. This time before Rev E. Powys, Mr J. Hulme, and Mr W.A. Coyney. Whether he appeared before them at their instigation or his own it is impossible to know, but this time he adds, '*The yard of Thomas James was in the privy parts of the ass the last time a minute and a half to two minutes, that he believes the yard of Thomas James dropped out of the she-asses privy parts of itself before Thomas James had seen Thomas*

Inskip and been interrupted by him...' and for a third time he puts his damning cross on the deposition.

In the Staffordshire Summer Assizes of 1811, among the 'Recognitions to Prosecute and Give Evidence', the name of Richard Jackson appears alongside that of Inskip, although Jackson never actually gave evidence or made a deposition. By the standards of today the whole thing seems incredible, but Thomas James paid for Inskip's persistence with his life.

The judges at the summer assizes of 1811 were Sir Soulden Lawrence and Sir Simon de Blane, and they considered Inskip's evidence to be '...*so clear and circumstantial'* that the jury, without hesitation, brought in a verdict of guilty.

Throughout the trial and right up to the moment of his execution poor Thomas James continued to denounce the character of the witness, but everyone took Inskip's word against that of James, and despite never having been in trouble before, the death sentence was pronounced.

Paradoxically, the two judges proved that they could be lenient. At the same assizes, two murderers received light sentences. John Clewlow was given six months imprisonment for killing Thomas Phillips at Stafford. Both were privates in the Eastern Regiment of the local militia. Thomas Phillips was drunk and in passing Clewlow's lodging house had shouted some sort of provocation. Clewlow had risen to the bait and rushing out of the house, had fought with Phillips and Phillips had knocked him to the ground.

Clewlow had gone back into the house and returned this time with a weapon, which was not even produced in court, with which he had hit Phillips, fracturing his skull. As a result of this injury Phillips died a few days later. Three respectable gentlemen gave Clewlow 'a good character' and he was therefore charged with manslaughter and given six months.

The next case of murder at these assizes was that of

twenty three year old S. Gee, who was given only *six weeks* imprisonment for killing John James, 'as a result of a casual battle', at Aldridge!

Other sentences imposed included transportation for seven years passed on William Edwards for stealing lime; William Marwood, for receiving lime, was transported for fourteen years; D.T. Sheriden for assault with intent to commit rape was sentenced to imprisonment for two years, '*... and to stand in the pillory at Stafford upon market day...*'.

Why then was poor old Thomas James given a capital sentence? There seems no logic to the judge's rulings. Several applications were made to procure his pardon '*... from consideration of the character of his prosecutor...*'.

It seems that Inskip had a dubious enough reputation for the defence to use it as a lever to get the sentence commuted, but to no avail. Thomas James was to pay the ultimate penalty, his family left to bear the ignominy and disgrace of the crime for which he was found guilty. The condemned man must have been concerned that this might ruin his chances of receiving a decent burial and told his wife that if she did not demand his corpse after his execution he would, if it were possible, *'visit her again.'*

Although he continued to refute utterly the charge and to '*..arraign the character of his prosecutor...*', even to the chaplain on the scaffold he was, towards the end, remarkably resigned to his fate. He walked firmly from his cell to the lodge where the scaffold was, but spoke to no-one else after the clergyman left him.

His wife and friends remained loyal, and as he had desired, they claimed his body and buried him with as much respect as their poor resources allowed.

Shaffalong

Eight
INCEST AND ABUSE
Joseph Preston of Shaffalong

Another sexual offence punishable by death was incestuous rape. Despite a plea for mercy made by his counsel, Congleton solicitor Mr Johnson, Joseph Preston of Shaffalong, near Cheddleton, on the outskirts of Leek was executed for this offence in April 1828.

By the standards of the time Joseph Preston had been fairly well placed. According to the Macclesfield press he possessed property in Macclesfield valued at £4500, but on his own admission he had led a dissolute life.

Forty eight years of age at the time of his trial, Joseph Preston maltreated his family to such an extent that his wife had left him. The children - Anne, John and Mary - had run away from their father on several occasions because of his ill treatment. They had been too scared to report him to the

47

authorities because of his threat to burn them alive if they did so.

After his wife had departed John Preston and his children lived at various locations. For several months the two girls had worked in one of the Macclesfield silk mills, but by 1826 they had moved to Shaffalong and were in such poor circumstances that they all slept on straw in the same room as their father. Mary was eleven, John fourteen and Anne sixteen.

It was during the corn harvest of 1826 that Joseph Preston turned his attentions to his youngest daughter and the little girl's evidence in court was confirmed by both John and Anne. The whole sorry case began to come to light when Anne ran away from home, stealing five shillings from underneath her father's pillow before running off to Brewood.

She lived in the area for six weeks, staying in lodging houses. When the five shillings was exhausted she began to earn her living from prostitution. She was brought before the local magistrate, E. Monckton Esq., in February 1827 as a common prostitute and for disorderly conduct at the Fleur de Lys in Brewood. She complained to the magistrate of ill treatment by her father as justification for her present circumstances, but she did not specify the precise nature of the alleged abuse. The magistrate awarded her two shillings out of the parish funds and advised her to return home, and that if she was further maltreated by her father to complain to the parish officers. The local constable, George Newman, who had arrested Anne at the Fleur de Lys said that as soon as she had received the two shillings from Mr. Monckton she went straight to the Gifford Arms and spent it all on drink.

Somehow Joseph Preston had discovered Anne's whereabouts and arrived in Brewood searching for her quite anxiously, according to some reports. He had even given two men a shilling each to help him to look for his daughter. He must have found Anne and taken her back home, for the next recorded event was that all three children fled, begging their way to Coventry. At Court House Green they all managed to find employment. Shortly afterwards Anne decided to try and seek out their mother and in May arrived in London, eventually locating her mother in Bethnal Green.

She poured out the story of their father's conduct towards Mary and herself. Preston had raped his eldest daughter in 1825 at a place called The Lloyd, a property he had acquired in Macclesfield as part of his wife's dowry.

Her mother took Anne to the attorney at the parish and then to the nearest Police Office where she made a formal complaint of Preston's ill-treatment of his daughters. She then sent to Court House Green for Mary.

Mary Preston was examined by a London surgeon, Henry Fuller, who established the fact that she had been violated and was also infected with a venereal disease of several months' standing.

Joseph Preston maintained that he was *'the most injured man in Staffordshire'* and recounted many instances of his wife's profligacy, firmly maintaining that the present prosecution had been instigated in order to regain possession of the property known as The Lloyd, which he had obtained upon marrying her. Several people came forward and gave Preston excellent character references, both for his kindness to the children and his general good conduct.

One relative, a Mrs Boughey, remembered quite distinctly that at Christmas twelvemonth both girls had told her, upon enquiry, that their father behaved as well to them as lay in his power...!

The judge summed up for an hour and a half. The jury consulted together in the box for ten minutes and then retired for half an hour before bringing in the verdict of guilty.

In the meantime, another jury had been sworn in and Joseph Preston was tried on a further indictment of raping his eldest daughter at The Lloyd in the summer of 1825. The long-suffering Anne was the only witness and was rigorously cross-examined for the second time. This time the jury took only twenty minutes to reach a guilty verdict.

The judge put on his black cap and addressed the prisoner:

'Joseph Preston, you stand convicted under two several indictments of the horrible, unnatural and incestuous crime of rape upon the bodies of two of your own daughters, the one under the age of eleven, the other under the age of thirteen, both the fruit of your own loins, bone of your bone and flesh of your flesh.

'The Act of Parliament for the transgression of which you are now called upon to answer has been in operation more than two hundred and fifty years, but I am persuaded that neither this nor any other court of justice in the kingdom ever witnessed during that long succession of years a spectacle so revolting to our nature and so harrowing to the feelings of those who are bound to dispense the criminal justice of the country as that which we have had the misery to witness this day.

The legislature never could have contemplated, when it passed the statute, the necessity of making provision for the protection of an innocent daughter against the worse than brutal violence of such a father, a father bound by the strongest ties of natural affection, of duty, and of moral obligation to instil into their minds those virtuous principles which in maturer life might arm them against the temptations and seductions of the world. Dead to all the social affections and to all the sympathies and charities common to our nature, instead of being the guardian of their innocence, you have been the despoiler of their chastity, and the corrupter of their virtue. Crimes so infamous and abominable can only be expiated by the blood of the offenders. You have justly incurred the penalty of death and it is my most painful duty to inform you that penalty will be most rigidly exacted. Let me implore you as you value your immortal soul to avail yourself of the spiritual assistance that will be afforded to you, and lose not an instant in preparing for the awful change which so speedily awaits you.

It remains only for me to pass the awful sentence of the law which is that you be taken from here to the place from whence you came and from thence to the place of execution there to be hanged by the neck until you are dead and may the Lord have mercy on your soul.'

According to newspaper reports of the trial, the judge appeared exhausted and quite overcome by emotion.

Preston groaned heavily during the sentencing. Until the moment of his execution he denied that he was guilty to the degree asserted by the witnesses. He acknowledged that he had indulged in an incestuous relationship with Anne, but *'with her consent and by her inducement...'.*

He positively denied every part of the charge relating to little Mary. His despicable attempt to try and justify his lust, and blame the whole thing on a thirteen year old girl did not do much to gain him public support.

Preston seems to have been a thoroughly unworthy specimen *'... possessing but a weak mind...',* and after doing untold damage to the lives of his wife and daughters he went to the gallows ' manifesting but little or no religious concern.'

Orgreave Cottage

Nine
A STAY OF EXECUTION
Thomas Bond of Orgreave

This is the story, not of a *stay* of execution for a criminal, but of an intended victim who was saved from death by her sturdy Victorian *stays*!

Situated one mile from Alrewas and two miles from Kings Bromley, in the early summer of 1895 Orgreave was a sleepy and picturesque rural community. Mr A Grossman lived at Orgreave Hall and the nearby Orgreave Farm was inhabited by a Mr P. Averill. Opposite stood a pretty cottage, the windows of the upper floor jutting through the tidy sloping thatched roof. The cottage had one large living room opening into a small grocers' shop, which in turn gave access onto the country lane separating the cottage from Orgreave Farm. The lane was merely a cul-de-sac leading only to the field which surrounded the back of the farm premises on the right and the yard and cottage on the left. About forty yards away, across the field, was the turnpike road.

In the cottage lived sixty six year old Mr Frederick Bakewell and his wife. Mr Bakewell was a small grocer cum farmer. It was not unusual for people to hold such dual occupations at this period. Staying with them for a short time was George Hackett, aged twenty eight, one of Mrs Bakewell's sons by a former marriage. A dark and handsome young man, George was employed as an under-guard with the Midland Railway Company. The cottage had been in the Bakewell family for a hundred years and the family was well known in the area as hard working and respectable. One of George's brothers, Charles Hackett, was a gardener at Orgreave Hall and another a wagoner at Little Bridgeford near Stafford.

At nine in the morning of May 31st 1895, Mr and Mrs Bakewell were sitting down to breakfast at a little round table in the inglenook. Mrs Bakewell was putting lump sugar into a basin when her son George came downstairs. Having just risen, he passed his mother on the way to the back door which was open, but he did not have chance to go outside for as he reached the door there was a loud explosion. George had been shot in the chest at close range with a repeating revolver.

He staggered back, screaming, and crossed the room to get to the other door. Before he could reach it he was hit by another shot.

Mrs Bakewell spun round to see a dark man come in through the door and approach the table where she and her husband were sitting. He shot Frederick Bakewell twice in the back and then shot Mrs Bakewell, but she was lucky, saved by her tight corseting of Victorian fashion. The bullet passed through her jersey and corsets and penetrated some wadding underneath, slightly injuring her breast. She reported later that she fancied that the man had shot at her again as she ran to her son.

She found George lying face down on the ground outside the front door. He was almost entirely lifeless. That

54

night as she undressed, the bullet fell from her clothing to the floor!

Living with Mr Averill at the farm opposite the cottage was his mother-in-law Mrs Barton, and at half past eight that morning she was in the first floor window watching Mr Averill go up the road on his way to Rugeley, en route to North Wales to attend to some business. As she waved him off, she caught sight of a man in the field among the trees behind the cottage. He appeared to be waiting for something - possibly for the menfolk to leave. He was about eighty or one hundred yards distant, but he must have caught sight of Mrs Barton in the window and endeavoured to step back out of sight.

When she went downstairs a little while later, she was suddenly startled by a commotion in the little cottage opposite. There were screams and shots and looking out she saw George Hackett stagger and fall outside the doorway. A moment later his mother rushed out and knelt beside him.

Also arriving to investigate the racket was another neighbour, Mrs Lester, who rushed into the cottage and tried to help old Mr Bakewell, but to no avail.

The murderer made off from the back door across the corner of the grass field which separated the open yard and the back premises of the house from the main turnpike road from Alrewas to Kings Bromley. He climbed over the palings into the road and was gone.

The police were called and instantly notified Stafford, Burton and Lichfield. Alarms were sent through all the surrounding countryside and villages and a search began.

Rumours suddenly abounded of a dark looking man who had been seen at various times and locations throughout the area over the preceding ten days. Mrs Bakewell's son-in-law, George Smith, said that a man had peered into his cottage window at Kings Bromley Wharf on Thursday, but his little son had called his mother - George Hackett's sister - and the man

55

took off.

The double murder appeared absolutely motiveless. Perhaps the murderer had expected to find the cottage empty and intended to rob it? Or perhaps he had heard that Mr Bakewell had sold some pigs to Mr Humphreys of Lichfield and had given his wife £5.16s. in silver?

Mrs Bakewell remembered that she had seen the man on a previous occasion, last Sunday week. She was known to give to beggars, and when a wretched, dark looking man had called asking if he could buy some milk she had refused to take the shilling which he had offered and had given him a drink. She had been particularly taken by his dark complexion and colouring and had engaged him in conversation asking 'Was he a native?', but he had answered no and gone away.

The police now knew immediately whom they wanted to interview. The description fitted that of a convict out on license, a convicted horse stealer and notorious house breaker, already wanted for failing to report back. They released the following description:

'Thomas Bond:
Age 30 years.
Height 5' 8"
Blue eyes, very dark hair and whiskers - which
latter may be now partly shaven off.
Very dark complexion.
Dressed in black cloth jacket,
sacque shape vest of the same material
and supposed dark brown corduroy trousers,
old canvas boots with india rubber soles,
round black hard felt hat,
linen collar and black necktie.'

The description rang a bell with Thomas Pendry, gamekeeper to Mr Grossman, whose cottage was about a mile away. Whilst checking on his brooding hens that morning at five to eight he had seen a man answering that description passing along the road which would take him to the scene of the murder. He had been wearing a black pilot coat and dark waistcoat with cord trousers and thick hobnailed boots. He had both hands in his pockets '......*as if he had hold of something...*' He was about 5'8" tall, with dark whiskers.

With such a dangerous murderer on the loose the whole county was in uproar. A photograph of Thomas Bond appeared in the Police Gazette and was extensively circulated. Police enquiries spread throughout Staffordshire and the adjoining counties.

The landlord of the Junction Inn, Kingswood, in the parish of Tettenhall, positively identified the picture of Thomas Bond as that of a chance customer who had come into his inn on the 1st of June. On June 3rd he had been seen at the Summer House Inn Boningdale, Salop. On the 4th at approximately 11.15 pm he had been found hanging around at the back of the inn and had been ordered off. Boningdale is only six miles from Bishopswood, near Brewood, where two attempts at robbery were made during the evening of June 4th.

The following night there were robberies at Moreton and Wilbroughton. The proceeds of one robbery yielded two guns and a quantity of powder and shot. On the following day, Thursday, a man whom Shropshire police were convinced was Bond was seen carrying a gun wrapped in oilcloth in the streets of Newport. The other gun was found by some boys in a field.

On Thursday evening at Hinstock, the house of a Mr Cooper was entered and ten pounds was stolen, one pound of which was in threepenny pieces. The police showed Bond's photograph, and several people identified it as that of a man seen around the Hinstock area earlier that day.

On Friday a man answering Bond's description went from Market Drayton railway station to Manchester paying his three shilling fare in threepenny pieces. He had booked to London Road, but got off the train at Longsight, two stations before London Road. The ticket was identified by Shropshire police.

Late on Saturday night at Baguley, about six miles from Longsight, a man armed with a revolver stopped two men and demanded money. One of them gave him threepence but the other struck up the gun with his stick and the man ran off. A little later he was seen going towards Manchester, then the trail stopped dead.

The police did not confine their search to one area. It was thought that Bond could be living rough in Needwood Forest, as he had managed to avoid capture in this way on a previous occasion, when wanted for horse stealing.

On the Thursday a report was received at Stafford that a suspicious looking man had been seen at Marchington near Uttoxeter. Inspector Templeton and nine men from Forebridge Barracks were dispatched instantly to investigate and carry out a thorough search of the area.

Mrs Bakewell continued to live in the cottage with two relatives for company. She told the police that she hoped that they would not catch him - *'I have quite forgiven him for what he has done.'*

Everyone was jumpy. Rumoured sightings of the murderer abounded. There was also a scurrilous rumour spreading that the shootings were actually the result of a family feud, but this was totally unfounded and caused even greater distress to Mrs Bakewell and her family.

On June 14th at 1.40pm, a telegram from Deputy Chief Constable Hallan of Nottingham police was received at Stafford. They had a man in custody. Instantly a policeman who knew Bond was dispatched post haste to Nottingham along with Inspector Nicklin of Burton.

By 1895 the advent of the telephone had considerably helped police procedure and the Nottingham police were able to telephone Stafford to report that Bond had been positively identified. He was carrying no weapons and nothing had been found to connect him with the Orgreave murders.

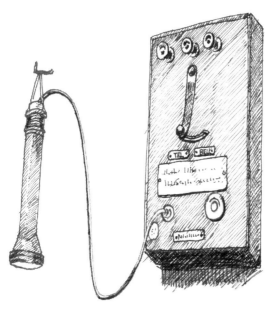

Now there were fears that what had seemed to be such a strong lead in Shropshire was going to prove worthless. The newspapers, however, having laid such emphasis on it in previous editions, were not going to give up so easily. *'The fact that the desperado who made his way to Lancashire bears a striking resemblance to Bond may yet be an element of importance...'*.

Bond had been captured at Hucknall Torkard by an extremely vigilant policeman who had arrested him on another occasion. The Nottingham police had been on the lookout for Bond for several days. Already convicted of burglary at a house in Newark and having served five years for the crime, he was already known to many of them.

Foolishly, Bond had walked past the police station in Hucknall Torkard and been spotted by the very policeman who had arrested him five years previously. Inspector Rushby remembered Bond because of his distinctive dark appearance. He ran out of the police station and arrested the wanted man.

Haggard and looking as though he had been living rough for several days, Bond admitted his identity. His clothes, not exactly as described by Staffordshire police, were tattered and he was very dirty. He was also found to be in possession of some articles of small value, the proceeds of a robbery committed at Mansfield the previous night, details of which had only been notified to the Hucknall Torkard police about two hours previously.

Bond was transferred to Burton-on-Trent and an identity parade was organised. Six men were fetched at random from the street and stood with Bond in the line-up. When Mrs Bakewell walked into the room she gave a sharp nervous glance along the line, sick at heart now that the time had arrived to meet the murderer of her husband and son face to face. When her eyes fell on Bond she gave a start and began to tremble uncontrollably. Despite her previous statement that she had forgiven him, she said in a low, clear voice, *'That is the villain,'* before turning away to hide her emotions as memories of that terrible day came flooding back. A policeman began to lead her gently away when she suddenly turned, as if about to rush at Bond. She was quietly restrained and led from the room.

Nine other people picked out Bond as the man they had seen in the Orgreave area during the few days preceding the murders. George Marler, a farmer at Parsons Brake, Hanbury, claimed that he had particular cause to remember him. On the afternoon prior to the shooting he had seen a man crossing his mowing grass at about half past one and anxious to stop him doing any more damage to the crop he had shouted after him, *'Come back! That is not your way!'*

The man had taken no notice, so George had called out to him again, but the man again ignored him. George began to run after him and as he reached the mowing field fence he shouted, *'If you don't come back, I shall fetch you !'*

At this the man turned and shook his fist at George. *'Come on then!'* he goaded.

'Oh, I'm not afraid of that, if that's your game!' Incensed, George had jumped the fence and made after him.

Indignantly, George told all who would listen to him that at that point the man drew a revolver from his breast pocket. *'... and before I could say Jack Robinson - he had a pop at me. Oh, that's your game is it?* said I, *then I'm off!* As I started to go I turned round and said, *All right my boy, I know you! You are Tommy Bond !'*

'Whereupon, he fired a second barrel at me and the bullet tore the fence just behind me. I then shot off as fast as I could and immediately reported the matter to the police.'

None of the witnesses from Shropshire and Lancashire who had identified Bond's photograph as that of a man seen loitering in their area were able to pick out Bond from the line up. An eye witness who saw the captured Bond on this day described him as *'A dark, ruddy complexioned young fellow, rather of the gipsy type, but by no means a repulsive looking man. He was wearing a light grey cloth cap, a short black coat bound with braid, dark brown cord trousers and thick boots. Despondent, but healthy and well.'*

By the time Bond appeared before the magistrates at Lichfield Guildhall he looked the worse for his short time in gaol, unshaven and very pale and his cheeks sunken.

A large crowd gathered outside the Guildhall on the day of the hearing. Bond arrived at Trent Valley station on the 11.03 am train, handcuffed to P.C. Davies. As they approached the Guildhall there were murmurs of *'..here he is...'*

On the whole there were none of the demonstrations which the police had feared, but some of the women in the crowd began to hurl abuse and invective at the prisoner. Mrs

Bakewell was well known in the area and the subject of much public sympathy. Bond was hurriedly ushered upstairs to where an old fashioned movable dock had been erected in the Hall.

Mrs Bakewell, her friends, witnesses and several leading citizens had been allocated seats in an enclosure railed off from the main body of the Hall. A crowd of several hundred people, whose behaviour was far from seemly, crammed against the barrier. The presiding magistrates were Mr A.E. Manley and the Mayor of Lichfield, Mr T. Walmesly. Mr A. Madan was also present during part of the proceedings.

Wearing a heavy widow's veil, Mrs Bakewell was seated very close to the dock. As the haggard looking Bond was led in and placed in the dock she raised the veil to look at him. The strain of the previous days had taken its toll and she was completely overcome. Losing control completely she tried to get to her feet, presumably in an attempt to physically attack Bond. Her friends were hard put to restrain her and with bitter tears in her eyes she cried, *'That's the man! That's the villain! I should like to have my revenge on you, you wretch!'*

Held down in her seat by her friends, Mrs Bakewell hardly took her eyes off Bond throughout the entire proceedings. The prisoner paid close attention to everything, especially to Mrs Bakewell's deposition which was read out by the Magistrates Clerk, Mr Thomas. The defendant was allowed to question Mrs Bakewell, and seemed intent upon trying to prove that she had made a mistake about the actual date he had called to buy milk. His voice was just a whisper, and his cross examination brief, Mrs Bakewell constantly reiterating, *'You did it! You are the man. You know you were there!'*

Bond was remanded for a week and taken on the 1.57pm train from Trent Valley to Stafford. He was given a substantial lunch of bread and cheese, and while the train was still in the station a young woman persisted in peering through the coach windows at Bond. He remarked to his escort that *'she might never have seen anyone before!,'* and cheekily blew her a kiss.

Bond had an impressive criminal record. Only thirty one years of age, he had spent the major part of his life in prison. Born the son of a labourer at Hixon, after several minor delinquencies, he received his first prison sentence at Derby Quarter Sessions on January 5th 1881 - nine months' hard labour for stealing four pounds and ten shillings. A catalogue of sentences followed and by the time he appeared at Lichfield Guildhall, Bond was in every sense of the word a hardened criminal. His record reveals a dismal career -

- At Stafford Quarter Sessions on October 16th 1882, two months' hard labour for housebreaking.

- January 1884 at Grantham House police court, fourteen days for begging.

- April 1884 at Stafford Quarter Sessions, twelve months' hard labour for a burglary committed at Tutbury.

- At Derbyshire Quarter Sessions on January 6th 1886, five years' penal servitude for horse stealing.

- On July 9th 1890, at Nottingham Assizes, another five years penal servitude for breaking into a house and stealing £1.3s.6d. and a watch.

When Bond was arrested for his last crime, he was also wanted by the Staffordshire police for stealing a colt and three heifers at Bradnop, near Leek. He sold the animals at Ashbourne, but was afterwards fleeced of his ill gotten gains by some ladies of ill-repute at Derby. From Derby he made his way to Abbots Bromley, entering two houses en route. He then visited a relative at Abbots Bromley who had turned him away, wanting nothing to do with him.

That night a valuable cart mare was stolen from the Reverend Provost Lowe. The mare was subsequently traced by Police Sergeant Hempton. She had been in Bond's possession and had been taken to Nottingham and sold for £38.0s.

Bond was then traced to Mansfield, where a horse belonging to a local medical man had been stolen. A man answering Bond's description had turned up at Newark market hoping to sell a horse, but on being closely questioned by a suspicious auctioneer the man abandoned the animal and made off.

He then committed the burglary for which he was arrested by Inspector (then Sergeant) Rushby, who also arrested him for the Orgreave murders.

At the time he killed the two men he was again wanted by the police, this time for failing to report himself. He had been released on a ticket-of-leave from Birstall Convict Prison on May 8th 1895. He went to St. Giles Mission, London, and they transmitted the eighteen shillings he had earned whilst in prison to the chief constable's office in Stafford. Bond collected his money there on May 9th.

After staying with his aunt at Hixon until May 15th, he then announced his intention of going to Lichfield in search of work. That night there was a burglary at Elmhurst, in the house of Mr Walpole. Bond was the prime suspect.

When Bond was committed for trial the hearing had to be held in the magistrate's room at Wade Street, Lichfield. There were few members of the public present because of the behaviour of the crowd at Bond's first hearing in the Guildhall.

The prisoner's father - who bore no resemblance to his wayward son - his sister and a female cousin were present at the committal proceedings, also his uncle and aunt from Abbots Bromley. Bond was obviously very pleased to see them there and nodded happily to them. He saw them again at the end of the hearing and his father, sister and cousin travelled with him on the train back to Stafford.

At Stafford he was met by his uncle, aunt and another

female relative. His aunt was very distressed and she grabbed hold of his free hand and clung to his arm as he was taken across the bridge to a waiting cab.

The trial produced a plethora of witnesses who testified to Bond's presence in the vicinity on the days preceding the murder. The defence countered that this only proved that Bond was a tramp. Mr Marler recounted his ordeal of being fired at by Bond.

The defence said Mr Marler was giving this evidence for dramatic effect - it was very strange that Bond should stay in the neighbourhood, if he had indeed shot at Mr Marler, then made an impassioned plea that unless the jury was absolutely sure that Bond was the murderer and not just a tramp, they should not give the verdict against him.

The prosecution, however, then produced twelve year old Walter Heathcote, who provided the clinching evidence against Bond. He had been on his regular early morning errand to fetch the family's milk and had seen Bond twice, the first time at 8.35 am on his way to fetch the milk. He had collected this, delivered a letter and then on his way back home had actually seen Bond in the act of approaching the back door of the Bakewell's cottage, immediately prior to the murders. Walter positively identified Bond and the defence could not produce any witnesses who had seen Bond anywhere else at the crucial time. The jury was out for only ten minutes before returning to pronounce Bond guilty.

The judge told him:

'Your object was, apparently, simply slaughter. The witnesses who traced you from the village where you slept the night before, up to the very door of the house, those who traced you back again until you went away and left the village after you had committed the dreadful deed, all testify to circumstances which leave no shadow of doubt in my mind that you are rightly pronounced guilty of this diabolical murder. The

law of this country knows no other punishment than that of death for the crime you have committed.'

As Bond turned to leave the dock he seemed completely unconcerned. He looked up into the gallery where his aunt and sister were sitting. They both stood up and blew him a kiss. He returned the greeting, then walked down to the cells.

On the day of his execution, 20th August 1895, several hundred people assembled outside Stafford prison. The executioner was Mr G.H. Scott of Huddersfield, a fair haired man of about forty years of age and of average build, wearing a blue serge suit and sporting a velvet cap. He had travelled down the previous day and stayed in the prison overnight.

By this date a couple of 'humanitarian modifications' had been introduced to the execution process. The noose had a leather surface to avoid unnecessary abrasion and when Bond mounted the scaffold, which was situated within a building in the courtyard, with folding doors resembling a coach house, he was placed with his back to the spectators. The newspaper commented: '

'This can only be a merciful dispensation alike towards the criminal and those whose painful duty it is to be present on such occasions. Formerly the culprit faced the spectators, and the dreadful expectancy written on the countenance before the blindfolding was a trying sight. The fall was followed by a quivering of the body and considerable vibration of the rope with faint gaspings from the culprit. The head appeared to be thrown back to an unusual degree exposing to view a neck and throat of muscular development. Consciousness, there is every reason to believe, had been lost from the moment of the fall, but the spasmodic movements continued for a minute or so longer."

With a drop of six feet, eight and a half inches, Bond's vertebral column was dislocated and death was instantaneous. After the execution Bond's final statement was released:

'It is my desire that this should not be known to the public until after my death. I am lawfully accused and condemned of the crime of wilfully murdering George Hackett and his stepfather. I beg of Mrs Bakewell and Mrs Hackett and those of whom I have injured by my crime to forgive me as I go to my death with my heart full of sorrow and ready to offer my life to God in atonement for these crimes. I also ask those whom I have injured by robbery to forgive me, especially my father, brothers and sister. I am fully convinced of the justice of my sentence and beg God to have mercy on my soul.'

Despite the fact that no Shropshire witnesses positively identified Bond, the police were still inclined to think that it had indeed been him, and that it would have been easy for him to travel from Manchester to Leeds and Sheffield, and that he had been relieved of the proceeds of his robberies in the same way that he had lost them before.

The suspicions of the police were reinforced by the fact that Bond was wearing a new cap, described in the previous eye witness report, which on his own admission had been purchased in Leeds.

The journey from Yorkshire to Northampton would have been simple enough, and the items found on him when arrested had been the proceeds of a robbery at Pleasley which lies near Mansfield and north of Hucknall Torkard.

Inspector Rushby of Northampton police received a reward of fifteen shillings for his vigilance in spotting and arresting Bond. The money was released from a fund at the disposal of Captain Anson, Chief Constable of Staffordshire, and was no doubt, a very welcome addition to the policeman's pay.

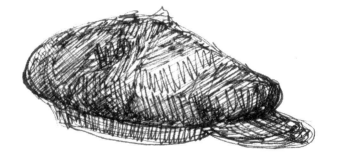

Ten
A FALSE NOTE.
George Fearns of Bottom House

Dealing in counterfeit bank notes was a very lucrative business, but to be caught passing a forged note was a capital offence. Many people chose to take the risk, however, and the whole business was a great problem to the law enforcement agencies.

The Bank of England had been tipped off that a certain George Fearns of the pub at Bottom House, about four or five miles from Leek, had been passing forged notes, and so they arranged for him to be investigated by an enthusiastic Manchester constable named Nadin.

On July 1st 1801, accompanied by P.C. Marshall Knowles, Nadin went to Bottom House and there proceeded to 'set up' George Fearns. They arrived at eleven at night, Nadin using the name River and Knowles using his christian name, Marshall. Both constables were disguised as hawking peddlers and carried a stock of cambrics, muslins and prints in a one horse chaise. As they seated themselves in the pub, Fearns came to serve them, but at this point the only conversation which passed between them was when Nadin observed, *'It's bad times and a man has fow werk* (hard work) *to live honestly.'*

Nadin and Knowles stayed the night and after breakfast the next morning Nadin ordered rum and milk. Assuming that if Fearns was indeed engaged in the passing of forged notes, he would probably be interested in other dishonest practices, Nadin then complained about the quality of the rum and asked Fearns from where it had been obtained. The reply was suitably vague - that it was from a man in Manchester.

Nadin intimated that he dealt in rum and could supply Fearns cheaply. Fearns said, *'I suppose you are a smuggler - but how can you afford it?'*

Nadin replied that the going rate was 6s. or 6s.6d per gallon. Scenting a fast profit Fearns immediately took the bait and promised to take any quantity Nadin could get for him. He was concerned to know how Nadin could deliver without the excise man discovering about it. Fearns was most impressed when Nadin explained that it would travel as flour - it was possible to hide a cask containing twenty or twenty one gallons in a barrel of American flour.

Nadin and Knowles then showed Fearns their goods, asking less than a quarter of their value, and Nadin said conversationally to Knowles, *'Marshall, when did that man say he would send the swag?'*

Fearns, catching on, said he supposed they were 'spoke to' (stolen), pointing to the goods, and Nadin admitted that was the case. During this conversation Nadin put down a forged Halifax one guinea note. Fearns spotted it instantly and said he was afraid he couldn't change it. Nadin said he only wanted him to look at it and say if it was not well done? Fearns was highly experienced in this field and said that he had seen that it was a forged one, and thought it was a bad one at that!

Feeling that he had his fish almost hooked, Nadin said, *'Marshall, where are the screeves?'*, all the time keeping an eye on Fearns, whose expression he noted changed from rather gloomy to *'quite licksome'*.

Passing forged notes afforded Fearns the opportunity to make even more money than selling smuggled rum. He must have felt that this fortuitous meeting with the peddlers could open many doors, but did not anticipate the particular door which finally swung ajar. Fearns began to become more talkative and said the 'screeve business' had been very good two or three years ago, but one Jackson had *'played the devil with it, he had quite spoiled it.'*

Trying to explore another lead which had suddenly presented itself, Nadin nonchalantly asked about Jackson's whereabouts.

'He is gone out of the country about some heifers.'

This would probably mean that he had travelled into another county, not country, unless he had gone to Ireland. The conversation continued on the subject of 'screeving' and Nadin produced some Bank of England notes which he had obtained from a forger in Chester, who had been transported for his sins. Fearns was not impressed, condemning them as badly executed.

Nadin vociferously defended them, saying that he had never seen better, thereby hoping to provoke Fearns into producing some of his own forged notes for comparison. He maintained that he had 'smashed' (passed) several and would no doubt pass many more. Fearns asked where he had obtained them and Nadin replied,

'From a man called Ben Baker but that he was at a loss to get any more as he had run away.'

'What did you give for a pound screeve?' asked Fearns.

'*8s.6d. for the £1.0s.0d. and 14s. for the £2.0s.0d.*'

'*That is the price I give for them, but you must not offer to smash any in Leek or Congleton or you would be leg'd* (caught) *directly!*'

Nadin said that he had smashed one at The Bull in Congleton!

'*It's a wonder you weren't leg'd! A man was taken up there* (arrested) *a little time ago who is now in Chester Gaol and has been snitching* (informing) *about me. The constable and cavalry from Leek have been and searched my house and several other houses round here that deal in the screeve way.*'
Forgery was obviously rife in the Leek Moorlands!

Fearns asked Nadin if he ever dealt in five or ten pound notes. Nadin replied that he never saw any, he wished he could get some, and then he'd go to Ireland and buy some salt beef and pork as he could pass any quantity there. Fearns thought this an excellent idea and said he didn't mind if he went with them!

Knowles, who had just been outside, returned at this point and told Fearns that there was a man at the door from Manchester. Nadin feigned concern urging Fearns not to let anyone in.

'*These goods are all spoke to and if anyone sees them I shall be taken up.*'

'*Nobody will come in here.*' reassured Fearns, '*And I will show you a five pound screeve before you go.*'

He went off for an hour to deal with the liquor merchant and came back with a five pound and ten pound note.'*These are articles - look at mine and look at yours!*' he said proudly.

Nadin said he'd never seen a five pound screeve and asked what he should give for one? Fearns said that he had given a guinea and a half for it. Then he was called away again and took the note with him.

Nadin began to feel that he might be losing his prey and that Fearns was not going to sell him any notes after all, so he 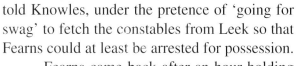told Knowles, under the pretence of 'going for swag' to fetch the constables from Leek so that Fearns could at least be arrested for possession.

Fearns came back after an hour holding two notes and Nadin, thinking they were two five pound notes, offered him three guineas. Fearns looked a rather taken aback and replied, *'Aye man, but one is a ten pound screeve!'*

Nadin agreed three guineas for the ten pound screeve and one and a half guineas for the five pound screeve and half a guinea for a one pound note.

Fearns pulled out a canvas bag from an inside waistcoat pocket, which contained a five pound and a one pound note. Nadin wanted to buy them, but Fearns refused, saying that he was going into Yorkshire soon, and could smash them for their full value. He warned Nadin not to squeeze or rumple the notes as the water mark was made with stiff material and would *'break all into pieces.'*

'These are a good sort.' he added, *'My brother Tom and I played the devil with them in Wales, where we smashed £500 worth. We bought horses and cattle which he then sold in Nottinghamshire. We had a license in horses. Do you know Long Tom?'*

'Do you mean Tom Markey?'

Fearns said he didn't know the surnames, but that was the man from whom he had had the notes. *'He comes here once a month, so he will be here in a week and you can have any quantity.'*

If only Nadin hadn't sent for the constables, he might have set up Long Tom as well, but at that moment Knowles arrived with the constables and Fearns was arrested. The following morning he was committed to the County Gaol by the Rev. E. Powys.

Because of the contrived way in which Fearns had been manoeuvred into selling the screeves, Nadin and Knowles underwent a very thorough and lengthy cross examination in court. Their stories did not vary. Knowles' version corresponded exactly with Nadin's and the defence could not shake their evidence.

An inspector from the bank, Mr. Glover, was brought in to prove that several bills purchased by Nadin from Fearns, and also those found upon Fearns by the constables, were indeed all forgeries.

Defence counsel tried to throw in a red herring and get Fearns off on a technicality, by objecting to the indictment on the grounds that the number of one of the notes was not under the figure of Britannia. Mr Glover said that it was only in the small denominations that the numbers were placed in that position. His Lordship was not having any of this. He rejected the objection as trivial and said counsel might just as well object to the figure of Britannia in the indictment not being a facsimile of that upon the note!

The defence tried again by saying the indictment was loosely worded, it being stated as a bank note without saying that it was a promissory note. His lordship said that the words of the relevant act were "bank note" and that was quite sufficient !

Fearns tried to deny everything, claiming that he knew nothing of the notes in question, he did not sell them, and furthermore had witnesses to prove that he did not.

James Bloor, a baker living near Bottom Inn said that

he had been there the whole time, that no such conversation as stated by Nadin and Knowles had ever taken place and no notes had been produced. Bloor maintained that he had reached Bottom Inn between one and two o'clock, just after his lunch and left again at 8.00 p.m. They had all stayed in the front parlour and no conversations had taken place. He was asked to describe Nadin and replied that he was *'a lusty man with a light coat.'*

Asked why he had spent all afternoon at Bottom Inn, he maintained that he had been waiting for one John Chadwick to whom he owed money for flour, but he had failed to turn up.

The prosecution wanted to know when he had last met Fearns' father or brother or servant? Bloor denied seeing them at any time during the last two or three weeks, indeed not since July 2nd. He said that he had been told to come to the court at Stafford by Fearns' attorney. He had met with the attorney two nights prior to the start of the trial and told him what he had to say. He had said nothing to anyone else; he was a perfect stranger to Stafford; he knew no-one else in the town. He was put up at The Trumpet Inn and was unaware that Fearns' father, brother and servant were also staying there. Five witnesses were called to testify to the good character of James Bloor.

Nadin was recalled to the witness stand and asked to describe what he had worn at Bottom Inn? He had been wearing a dark brown coat was the reply.

Had he seen Bloor before?

No, he had never seen him, except here in the court, and with Fearns's father and servant on Thursday, and with Tom Fearns more than twenty times in total the previous day in the vicinity of The Trumpet. Knowles was re-examined and confirmed everything that Nadin had said.

Thomas Kent, owner of The Trumpet, was called. He confirmed that Bloor, Mr. Fearns senior, Tom Fearns and their servant were all in The Trumpet on Thursday, and that Bloor had supper with Tom Fearns on Thursday night, and that they had shared the same room on both Wednesday and Thursday nights. Kent's servant, Margaret Brown, confirmed this.

Bloor was not a cautious or sensible man. He was called again and stated his case as before. The jury found Fearns guilty and Bloor was rewarded for his pains with a charge with perjury.

In passing sentence the judge said that the crime proscribed any mercy. Paper credit was *the security of the affluence, riches and power of the country, and if forgeries were so frequent, and were so good, they must be stopped or there would be an end to commerce and an end to this country.'*

Forgeries, he maintained, affected the security of people like no other crime. A person could bar doors and windows; he could carry a little to minimise the risk of being robbed, but no one could defend himself against forgery. The judge then turned to the subject of Mr. Bloor, informing the court that he liked perjurers no more than he liked screevers. Another bar to mercy, he continued, was the introduction of a wilful perjurer in such an impudent and shameful way. The law must take its course.

George Fearns was executed on August 8th 1801, for uttering three bills knowing them to be forgeries of the Bank of England. With him on the gallows were T. Spittle, aged twenty three years, executed for stealing a horse valued at ten pounds, *'which he maimed in a most barbarous manner and afterwards sold for 14s.6d. ',* J. Smith, aged nineteen, *'for stealing a horse the property of his late master',* J.Harper, aged thirty years and John Palmer, aged thirty years for stealing a chestnut mare the property of a Mr Powell at Sedgeley. There was also another indictment extant against these two for stealing a black horse the property of Joseph and John Mills.

Thomas Fearns, George's brother, was committed for trial for uttering forged notes. He was sent to Ruthin Assizes as that was the area in which he and George had reputedly *'smashed their £500 worth of screeves'*, but despite having the same prosecuting officer as George, Tom was acquitted.

On April 3rd 1802, at the Stafford Assizes, James Bloor was sentenced to be transported for eight years for his perjury. He was transported in July 1802, and no doubt spent many a miserable hour cursing the name of Fearns and his involvement in the case. Had Fearns not tried so hard to mislead the court, the Judge may not have been so incensed, and may possibly have given a lighter sentence. Perhaps Fearns cursed Bloor's involvement just as heartily.

in front of the county Prison, at Stafford. Sat 17th Aug 1844

Eleven
A FORGED DEED
John Highfield of Mill Meece

It was not only banknotes that were forged, but also documents, to enable unscrupulous individuals to acquire land or other property. 1828 saw some Stafford constables having a very hard time trying to arrest John Highfield of Mill Meece for forgery.

The three constables had gone along with a magistrate's warrant to arrest John Highfield on a charge of forgery. He was staying at his son's house at Johnson's Wood near Market Drayton, then in the county of Stafford. Two of the constables, John Tooth and Edward Simister were disguised as drovers.

There was such a scrap that his children Matthew, Thomas and Sarah Highfield ended up being charged with assaulting Robert Jones, John Tooth and Edward Simister whilst performing their duty as constables, and effecting the rescue of John Highfield their father plus a charge of common assault.

When they drew near to the house, Robert Jones sent the other two ahead, beause he was known to the Highfields, to ask if they had any fat pigs to sell. They approached the barn and saw John Highfield senior and junior, and Matthew and Thomas.

Indicating the old man, John Tooth said to Simister, *'That's the man we want,'* and Simister approached the old man.

Realising they were not the drovers they had appeared to be from a distance John Highfield grabbed a threshing flail and struck out at Simister, catching him a severe blow on the neck.

As Simister dropped like a stone, Tooth was telling the old man that they had a warrant for his arrest. Matthew joined in, striking Simister with a fork as he lay helpless, and then ran away. Fearing for his comrade's life, Tooth shouted with an oath, *'Don't murder the man.'*

When John Tooth grabbed Highfield by the lapels, the old man, struggling like an eel, yelled to his dogs. *'Seize him, Bob!'*

Young John Highfield then attacked Tooth with a staff shouting, *'Let him alone!'*

Still grappling with the old man, Tooth shouted to him to *'........ shut up or he'd blow his brains out!'* Young John then managed to throw Tooth to the floor and old Highfield took off as fast as he could to the house. As Edward Simister began to gather his wits he became aware that John junior was holding on to Tooth and two large dogs were trying to worry him. His staff and pistol had fallen to the ground. When it became obvious that Simister was about to rejoin the fray John took off after his father to the house.

The three constables then pursued the disappearing Highfields, and reached the house to find the door firmly closed against them. They shouted to young John to open up, to which he retorted, *'Break it down if you dare! If you touch it I will knock you down!'*

Tooth fetched a spade and they forced the door open. Upon entering the house they saw John, Thomas and Sarah. They eventually ran the old man to ground hiding in a kind of garret to which there were no stairs. He had armed himself with some kind of weapon which he kept swinging at the constables every time they tried to get up to him.

Eventually Jones went to get help, leaving Tooth and Simister to keep an eye on the old reprobate. When he got back with the reinforcements, he found the other two constables out in the garden. Young Tom was now armed with a gun.

Jones warned that if the door was not opened, they would break it down. They went off and fetched a ladder from the rick-yard and used it as a battering ram to break in the door. The door burst open and out tumbled several Highfields and two dogs and a general fight ensued, with young John the principle assailant. One dog worried Simister continually, all the constables were hurt to some degree and old Highfield escaped into the night.

All the Highfields were eventually apprehended after a great deal of effort on the part of the constables. Old Highfield had managed to bolt as far as Halmerend.

Despite the fact that they had shouted, *'What? Have you come to steal the geese?'* as an excuse for setting the dogs on the constables, they were found guilty of assault and received a variety of sentences, from Sarah Highfield who was fined ten shillings and discharged, to young John Highfield who received a total of eighteen months' imprisonment. All this disturbance was because of the forgery of a deed of gift, in an attempt to acquire a parcel of land which they rented, upon the death of the owner.

Arrested with the Highfields as an accessory was a man named Charles Brown, but he turned King's evidence, so only John and William Highfield were placed at the bar, charged with '....*feloniously forging and uttering as true a certain deed of gift purporting to be a deed of one Joseph Ward with intent to defraud Joseph Peake son of the nephew of the said Joseph Ward.*'

Joseph Ward was a respectable farmer who lived at Mill Meece. With considerable property to his name he made a will, in 1817, leaving a small estate called Bowers to his nephew, Joseph Peake. John Highfield was tenant of this property, and he claimed some sort of relationship with Mr. Ward. In July 1819, aged eighty, Joseph Ward died, and when Joseph Peake claimed his inheritance, both he and the Ward family were surprised to find that the will was being contested by John Highfield on the basis of a deed of gift given by the deceased. They were particularly surprised, since Joseph Peake had spoken to John Highfield in the month of Mr. Ward's death, and no mention had been made then of any deed of gift.

The whole matter was taken before the court of chancery in an attempt to have the deed set aside as having been obtained by fraud, but as the case progressed, the circumstances seemed so suspicious that it began to seem that not fraud but forgery was involved.

As the evidence unfolded it appeared that forgery had been in Highfield's mind for some time. In the summer of 1818 he had offered the sum of one hundred pounds to Mr Lockley, a clerk in Mr Ward's attorney's office, to draw up a deed of gift from Mr Ward to himself, but Lockley had refused. Highfield had then approached in turn a man named Manley and an attorney by the name of Rolls in Newcastle. He had finally succeeded with Mr. Preston, an attorney at Burslem. Charles Brown was asked by Highfield to witness this document and did so, but subsequently, getting a case of cold feet, he had his name erased.

Some effort was made to discredit Charles Brown. He was accused of giving his damning evidence for the sum of three hundred pounds, given to him by John Peake, Hannah Ward and Sarah Peake.

Mrs Hodson, the wife of John Hodson of Walk Mill, near Eccleshall, was at Mr. Ward's home during his last illness and remembered John Highfield and a servant named Sarah Baggaley visiting Mr. Ward. Being rather infirm at this time of his life, Mr Ward was in bed. John Highfield had approached him carrying a roll of paper.

Sarah Baggaley went to the old man and said, *'Here is Mr. Highfield come to see you and ask how you do?'*

'Who?' asked the old man.

'Mr Highfield, who brings you the fish. You know, he is come to shake hands with you.'

``*I shall not shake hands with him, nor none such a damned rogue as he is!'*

Sarah then took the old man's hand and tried to pull it out of the bedcovers. Mr. Ward became very angry, threatening to dash her brains out if he could get to her with his stick!

John Highfield said, *'I'm afraid we shall do no good now with the old man, he has gone into such a passion.'*

Despite the fact that several people gave evidence that Mr Ward had treated John Highfield kindly, and a Mr Mansley gave evidence that he had spoken to Charles Brown in a pub and that Brown had told him that he had been offered three hundred pounds to say the deed was forged, the jury took only ten minutes to find John and William Highfield guilty, with a recommendation of mercy for William. As the judge put on his black cap, John Highfield pleaded with him not to do so, but he condemned them both to hang.

A contemporary account of Highfield describes him as *'a very robust man with a cunning expression of countenance'* and that he *'conducted himself with great firmness throughout the trial, paid great attention to the proceedings, and with uncommon self-possession, arising, it is said, from a natural insensibility, employed himself in writing suggestions to his solicitor on scraps of paper.'*

His brother William is described as having *'a stupid, senseless countenance.'* He seemed more humbled but appeared to understand little of the proceedings.

John Highfield remained unrepentant, the whole family insisting that the Deed was a true one. His wife declared of the death sentence, *'Well, it's a wrong thing, but I can't help it and I'm sorry for it.'*

One daughter told her father that as the executioner was entitled to his clothes, *'... if I were you, when I went up to be hanged, I'd pull all my clothes off but me breeches and go up naked.'* Sensitivity was not a Highfield family attribute!

Because of such statements the governor and magistrates banned visits to Highfield for several days. John Highfield maintained he would *'...die like a Mon...'* and that he *'would not have much meat for the two or three last days and then his body would keep better.'*

William Highfield's sentence was commuted to transportation.

As John Highfield awaited execution he spent much of his time writing, handing out several documents on his family's last visit. His 'Last Confession', denying everything, appeared in the Staffordshire Advertiser. He describes himself as *'This John*

Highfield about fifty six years of 'is age and Stands Two Yeardes hie, very lusty man as aney in the Countey, very Cliver and Stout in every thing as any one man Can be, and so you will Find Him to Die.'

On another document he wrote, *'On the sixteen of August I must Die by the neck 1828, my farther was marred that day and I was marred on third Day of August in 1793, and Died Wrong for that Crime...*

The turnkeys as my Garters and my Backer Box my silk ancher and coton hancher ould one, and my pocket knife and my spoon led one I.H. mark. And I Desire my wife will take them Hom with her and keep them for my Sack. Ould pare of stockings, 2 ould smock frocks, and my Cloas on my Back.

On the sixteen of August I must Die and you John Highfield you must Berry me som whare you Please. I should like you for to fetch a load of flags from Chaplin Charlton and lay them upon me same as Wm. Alsop of Coats Lodge. You must ask John Bedson how he was Berred. I should like to be berred has he was and take me to the Waggon to the Cheorch Yeard or you will ofend me very much. I Desire You Do So.

My son John Highfield. When my Brother Will. H. Go of I Desire you will let him hav som money before he Go of. The wont tell him before that night he Goes...'

John Highfield was the last person to be hanged at Stafford Gaol for forgery, and he was executed in the same week as the murderer of Maria Marten, the celebrated case which became known as the " Murder in the Red Barn."

Although stumbling on the scaffold he said to one of the attendants, *'Help me up, there's a good lad. I'll go like a MAN, like a LION.'*

He was dead within two minutes of the drop falling. There then followed a further disturbance when one of the daughters attempted to prevent an age-old custom from taking place. There was a belief at that time that having an executed man's hand drawn across the face cured skin complaints. A group of women had travelled a considerable distance to try and effect this 'cure' and were allowed to have the dead man's hand drawn across large wens on their necks. The daughter was desperately attempting to stop this, telling the officers that if they would not cut down the body, she would, *"...along with other shameful language.'* Because of this outburst she was refused permission to enter the prison when the body was put into the coffin.

It was later discovered that John Highfield had attempted to cheat the gallows. Blood was found on his collar and there were cuts to his throat. A search of his cell produced a shattered ink bottle, and it seemed he had attempted to cut his own throat.

His coffin was placed in a three horse wagon. His daughter spread a white cloth over the coffin, covered it with straw, sat herself down on it and rode off through the crowd, *'without any sign of grief.'*

Twelve

A SORRY END

Ann Statham of Wychnor Bridges

Undoubtedly, some of the crimes contained in this book would not even carry a prison sentence today, and the thought that in the past many have been executed for comparatively trivial offences is chilling indeed. A case in point is that of Ann Statham of Wychnor Bridges, near Burton on Trent.

The courts saw many cases of unfortunate girls who had, under the direst of circumstances, killed their babies. There was no mention then of post-natal depression, and many of these girls were hanged, including Ann Statham.

Ann lived with her mother at Wychnor Bridges. The house was about thirty yards from the mail coach route and Ann met Thomas Webster, the mail coach driver who took the Birmingham to Sheffield mail coach between Birmingham and Derby.

The relationship blossomed and Ann went off to Birmingham to live with Webster and stayed there for about ten months. She soon became pregnant, and as the date of her confinement drew near she moved to Derby.

When the baby was about five weeks old, she decided that she wanted to go and stay with her mother at Wychnor and so accordingly, on July 23rd 1816, Thomas Webster brought her from Derby on the mail coach to Burton, where she wanted to be left as she wished to see the constable, Mr Mason.

Webster next saw her the following day near her mother's and asked her how she was as he passed her. He did not see her again until Saturday July 27th, when he picked her up on his coach as he drove from Burton, and took her to the Three Tuns public house at Barton Turnings. They went into the pub together, and he asked how she and the baby were, and where it was. She replied that it was dead.

Webster was shocked and asked how this could be as the baby had seemed so well the previous Tuesday. Ann replied that it had died of a fit, or had died suddenly. Webster could not remember which when he gave evidence.

She told him that the child was to be buried at Walton, and wanting a decent burial for the child, Webster had volunteered to pay the expenses, asking Ann if she needed money. She replied that she did not.

In his evidence he said that he had always looked after her well and had treated her kindly, she had always seemed affectionate towards the child, and that he was able and willing to provide for them both. The next time he had called at the Three Tuns was on Sunday 28th when he saw the body of a child lying in the warehouse. It had been pulled out of the canal and he was unable to identify it positively.

Ann Statham had obviously not been herself. On her way from Burton to Wychnor she had met, at Branstone, a butcher from Burton named William Challinor. She spoke to him and asked him how he was, but he had not at first recognised her *'as she looked so ill.'* She explained that she had been lying-in at Derby and showed him the baby, asking him who he thought it looked like and explaining that it was Webster's child. He described the baby as *'a nice fat jolly well-looking child.'* She told Challinor that she was on her way to her mother's, but that she was badly tired. He suggested that she hitch a ride on a wagon which was at that moment passing, but she refused. Mary Palmer, who kept the turnpike gate near Branstone, was the next to see Ann when she stopped to rest at her house.

There were two roads from the turnpike gate, one the turnpike road going to Wychnor Bridges, the other leading for a quarter of a mile down to the canal. Ann took the road to the canal, and Mary shouted after her that she would do better to go down the turnpike road as a chaise had gone from Lichfield to Burton which she expected back at any moment, and she would be able to ride home. Ann said she preferred to go down by 'the cut' because she might light on a boat - the driver of the returning chaise would expect something for carrying a passenger, and a boatman would charge little or nothing. Mary Palmer said it was *'ten to one'* against her meeting a boat, but Ann was adamant that she would not wait for the chaise, but was going down by the canal.

John Deakin was employed as a boatman on the canal and saw Ann wearing a dark dress standing by the side of the canal between Branstone Bridge and the Three Tuns. She was near to a bridge called the Turnover Bridge, where the towing path changed from one side of the canal to the other. He noticed that she was suckling a child at her left breast, and she had two bundles lying beside her, one in a yellow silk handkerchief, the other in a whitish handkerchief. Another boat, steered by

George Thomas was alongside his own. They both proceeded to the Three Tuns, opposite, where they were to stay for the night. About an hour later, Ann Statham came up to where the boats were tied up. It had been raining heavily for three quarters of an hour and Ann appeared to be soaked to the skin.

George Thomas said to her '*You seem, mistress, to be sadly wet.*'

She said '*yes*' and he added, '*I thought of asking you to ride but I did not know which way you were going.*' She said it '*did not signify*' for she had to call at a little house by the roadside and she had left the child there for she '*dared not bring it forward for fear it should be wet.*'

Upon cross-examination of the two boatmen, the defence elicited the information that the tow path had partially collapsed and fallen into the canal a few yards from the place where they had seen Ann standing. She would have had to cross at this point in order to reach the Three Tuns. In the heavy rain the place would be even more wet and slippery.

On Tuesday July 23rd, between five and six in the evening, Mr Hodson of Barton was travelling on the turnpike road near Turnover Bridge when he noticed a woman in a dark dress by the side of the canal. It was raining very heavily and the woman had attracted his attention because she walked very slowly and paused frequently. She was about fifty yards from him and he could not swear positively that it was Ann Statham, but she was wearing a dark dress and carrying two bundles, one of which appeared to be white and the other of a different colour.

On Sunday, July 28th at about six in the morning, Thomas Wootton, a boatman, was travelling down the canal. Noticing something floating in the water about one hundred yards below Turn Over Bridge, Thomas steered his boat towards it. He fished the object out and saw that it was a baby boy, dressed in a white bed-gown and cap, and quite dead. He took it to the Three Tuns and left it there with the landlady, Sarah Tompson. Charles Nicholls, the constable of Barton was called and saw the body at about 7.30 a.m. Suspicion instantly fell on Ann Statham.

He went to her mother's where he found her having breakfast. When she saw the constable she became very agitated. He asked her where the baby was and she told him that it was at Derby, about sixteen miles away.

Constable Nicholls said, '*I mean the child which you were suckling on the towing path by the canal side on Tuesday last when the boats came past you, and after that you came by those boats at the Three Tuns and on being asked what you had done with it, you said that you had left it at a small house. THAT is the child I mean.*'

'*My child is at Derby.*'

Her mother then said, '*Ann, you always told me your child was at Derby.*'

'*I did leave it there, mother.*'

The constable was not convinced and took Ann into custody.

Mrs Tompson, whose husband kept the Three Tuns, confirmed that the child had been brought to her that Sunday morning and that later, when Ann had arrived, she had said to her, '*Ann, it is a pity that you did not come up by one of the boats that night.*'

'*I wish I had, and brought my baby with me; I had a fit and it fell out of my hands into the canal.*' She then put her hand to her knee. '*I waded after it as far as here, but could not reach it.*'

Mrs Tompson said that she had known Ann for several years but had never known her to suffer from fits.

Witnesses said that when Ann saw the baby with mud clenched in his tiny fists '*she fell down almost fainting.*'

On Tuesday, August 8th, Charles Nicholls junior took Ann to Stafford. As they approached the town she asked him,

'Do you think I shall be hung?'

He replied that he could not tell.

'I should think they cannot hang me, for no-one saw me.'

'I think you cannot tell, for there might be those eyes upon you that you could not discern.'

'I am sure there was not. I looked round, and there was no one by, nor anyone near.'

She did not say anything about a fit.

In his summing up Mr Justice Park emphasised Ann Statham's contradictory statements. That she had left the baby at a small house; that it had died in a fit, or suddenly; that it was at Derby; and that she had dropped it into the canal whilst she was in a fit.

If it had been an accident, why not run after the boatmen? Why not call to the gentleman who had been passing? He then drew attention to the conversation she had with Charles Nicholls junior, which he had found particularly damning. He told Ann that all murder was heinous, but there were gradations even in this, and hers was of the worst nature for she had killed her own offspring with no apparent motive. There was not even the motive of shame, as everyone knew of her cohabitation with Thomas Webster, who was willing and able to have provided for her and their son. No other motive could be assigned than that arising from a cruel, hardened and vicious disposition.

At the same assizes three other women, Mary Ray, Sarah Lowe and Elizabeth Barnes, were all tried for the murder of their illegitimate children, and all three were acquitted. A total of seventeen prisoners were given the death sentence at these assizes, but before he left Stafford the justice reprieved all except Ann Statham.

The poor woman, whilst acknowledging her guilt, needed the support of two men on the gallows. This was to be the last execution to take place on the top of the Lodge.

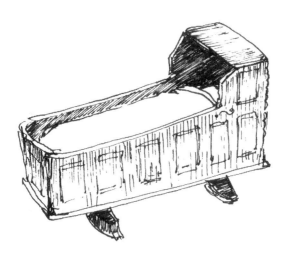

Thirteen
A Fatal Pregnancy
John Gould of Alstonfield

Another sad case was that of twenty three year old John Gould of Alstonfield, executed in 1811 for the murder of his wife Elizabeth.

John and Elizabeth had married early, their only means of support being whatever he earned from working for his father on his small farm in Alstonfield. Life must have been hard, and when his wife discovered she was pregnant with their second child, John Gould tried to abort the baby by rolling on his wife in bed and elbowing her in the stomach and crushing her. He succeeded in his attempt - but his young wife also died.

The defence brought forward Gould's sisters who tried to explain that the bruising and damage to Elizabeth's abdomen and uterus were caused by her falling over a wall, the stones of which collapsed upon her, but they contradicted themselves and only succeeded in arousing the prejudice of a court which might have otherwise been disposed to leniency on account of his pathetic circumstances. The jury took a long time to reach a guilty verdict and were obviously distressed by the details of the case. As the judge pronounced the death sentence Gould cried *'I am murdered!....'*

Gould's pathetic sobs were heard by all the prisoners in the gaol. As he awaited his fate he was inconsolable, and on the day of the execution he had to be forcibly removed from his cell. He was heaved up onto the gallows *'from which his cries were heard by a numerous and sympathizing populace to a considerable distance....and he appeared to die harder than most...'* Gould was *'.. a fresh complexioned young man, middle sized with a countenance not at all indicating hardness of mind, and expressive only of youthful rusticity...'*

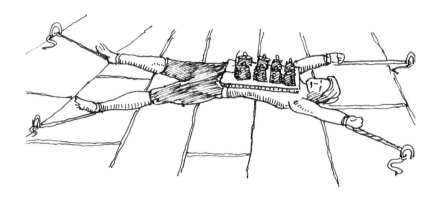

Fourteen
PEINE FORTE ET DURE
Nathaniel 'X' of Cannock

Horrific though it was to die on the gallows, worse methods than hanging were employed in Staffordshire to dispatch a criminal.

Peine forte et dure was a legacy from our Norman conquerors. Literally translated it was a sentence to be pressed to death and must surely be the origin of the expression 'hard pressed'.

Until relatively recent times, if a man was arrested for a crime there was every inducement for him to refuse to plead to the indictment. If he did plead and was found guilty, his whole estate became forfeit to the crown, and this meant that even his wife and children would be deprived of any means of support. If, therefore, a man did not wish to create a desolate future for his family, he kept quiet when asked how he pleaded. This was called 'standing mute of malice' and there was an official sentence to deal with such an occurrence:

'That the prisoner shall be remanded to the place from

whence he came and put in a low dark room and there laid on his back without any manner of covering except a cloth around his middle and that as many weights shall be laid upon him as he can bear and more and that he shall have no more sustenance but of the worst bread and water and that he shall not eat on the same day on which he drinks, nor drink on the same day on which he eats and he shall so continue until he die.'

The suffering could be intensified by a sadistic executioner, who placed a sharp stone underneath the body.

This barbaric sentence was abolished in 1772. One of the last culprits to be pressed was a highwayman who was reputed to have borne 350 lbs., but at 400 lbs he begged to be allowed to plead. He was accordingly taken back to court, found guilty and hanged at Tyburn in 1721.'

In the William Salt Library at Stafford there is a picture of 'Nathaniel...', suffering the sentence of *"peine forte et dure."* The picture seems to have been adapted from one depicting the pressing of Spiggot, a notorious seventeenth century criminal.

Not much is known about Nathaniel "X". His crime was supposed to have been so abysmal that the writer of the broadsheet, which is our sole source of information, was loath to give him immortality by using his real name and referred to him only as Nathaniel. Even the writer seems not to be sure of the date of his trial, but says he was arraigned at Staffordshire assizes in March 1674-5. His crime was the murder of his wife and both her parents in order to gain control of their meagre estate. Unfortunately it has proved impossible to locate the records of his appearance, so I have a nagging suspicion that this could just have been a ploy to sell broadsheets, but here is the story anyway !

Born in Cannock in the mid seventeenth century, Nathaniel came from a good family. Unfortunately his father died while Nathaniel was still young and the boy was allowed to run wild, both as a child and as a young man. He managed to find employment for himself as a servant to an honest and upstanding family with only one daughter, to whom Nathaniel, with an eye to the material prospects, began to pay court. This was solely for gain as he already had a sweetheart with whom he was in love. He had fallen out with this lady and had gone off and worked as a servant in several places, but *'by his flashing, lying and prodigally living above himself - which is the ruin of many, he could not stay long in any service so that he was reduced to a very low and sad condition.'*

Nathaniel evidently liked to live it up and in order to maintain himself in the manner to which he would like to become accustomed he set-to with a will to win the hand of his employer's daughter, *'who did not perceive his crocodile nature.'*

To please their only daughter her parents consented to the marriage, taking the reprobate Nathaniel into their home and treating him as their son.

Nathaniel was acquainted with a woman of ill-repute who lived just outside Cheslyn Hay. She had a very bad reputation among her neighbours, but Nathaniel had worked with her daughter at one of his places of employment, and it is also thought that this young lady had tried to help him with problems relating to his true sweetheart, prior to his marriage. For whatever reason, Nathaniel was often to be seen at Cheslyn Hay.

On one of his visits to The Hay to fetch a load of coal with his father-in-law's team, he had taken along his father-in-law's grandson. As was usual he called in to see the lady and she asked him who was the boy.

The two of them, then and there, concocted a scheme to poison the grandson, Nathaniel's wife and his parents-in-law and so be sole heir to their possessions. Once the idea was planted Nathaniel couldn't wait to put it into operation.

On the fifteenth day of January 1674-5 Nathaniel turned up in a mercer's shop in Penkridge and tried to buy a pennyworth of arsenic or 'ratsbane', as it was more generally known. The shopkeeper had none, but tried to sell him some brandy or tobacco instead. Nathaniel went off empty handed. There was another gentleman in the shop and so suspicious had Nathaniel looked that the shopkeeper was moved to comment to the other customer that '.. *this fellow looks as if he would poyson himself...*' and wondered who he was. The customer was able to tell him. Nathaniel had been a servant of his father's and was well known to the family.

Nathaniel managed to buy his ratsbane at another shop and the following Sunday put his plan into action. He put some of the arsenic into a dish of milk which was intended for the grandson, but he was late home that day, having gone off to play with some other boys after evening prayer.

His wife decided to make some toast and put it into the milk. This was a common dish in the household (and was still so in Staffordshire until well into this century), known variously around the county as 'soaky' or 'slops'.

Whether it was because Nathaniel could not bear to watch or not, is not revealed, but whatever the reason, when his wife had consumed about half the dish, he went outside to the barn, but '...*came back speedily being frightened by a black dogg which fastnd suddenly upon him*'. He sat beside his wife, who was still eating the poisoned milk, and as a ploy he suddenly feigned sickness.

The poor victim soon began to feel violently ill with severe vomiting and diarrhoea. She was in dreadful pain and suffered the symptoms all through Sunday night until she finally died at five o'clock on Monday morning.

Despite her suffering she managed to show a great deal of affection to her undeserving husband, although it was strongly believed that he continued to administer the poison to her in drinks throughout the night.

The next person to die was his mother-in-law, exhibiting the same symptoms as her daughter. On Wednesday his father-in-law died after taking some possett to which Nathaniel had added arsenic. Thursday saw all three corpses buried in the same grave in Cannock churchyard.

Nathaniel very nearly claimed another victim when the old man's nephew visited and ate some of the poisoned possett. Luckily for him he began to feel ill immediately and went home. Hearing of his indisposition a neighbour went to visit him, '... *and gave him sallet oyl and other things so that by that means and the help of doctors he is like to recover, but the poison broke forth with blotches and boils...*'

The three sudden deaths were the talk of Cannock and formed part of after dinner conversation at a gathering attended by the very young man who had witnessed Nathaniel trying to buy ratsbane in Penkridge. He wrote instantly to his brother-in-law about his suspicions, wondering what he should do, and the brother-in-law immediately informed *'some person of quality in the town'*, who immediately apprehended Nathaniel on suspicion.

After his arrest he was kept in close confinement, and suddenly in the middle of the night began to show signs of a fit. The keepers thought he had poisoned himself. However, he was merely intent on embroiling the woman from Cheslyn Hay.

'....*but recovering he confessed that that naughty woman had bewitched him to commit this horrid fact after which confession he fell into another exstasie in which his tongue was thrust out of his mouth insomuch that they could by no means thrust it nor keep it in.*'

The woman was arrested and brought to Cannock at about nine in the morning on the following day and as soon as Nathaniel was told that she was near, his tongue miraculously returned to its rightful place.

He then fixed the door by which she would enter the room with a fierce expression and fell upon his knees, praying to God to forgive all his sins. As soon as the woman entered he flew at her, and had to be pulled off, saying *'Oh thou base woman, thou hast utterly undone my poor soul and brought a disgrace upon my friends and relations.'*

The same day the coroner and jury ordered the bodies to be exhumed, and arsenic was found in all three, but most in the stomach of his young wife. Nathaniel confessed to the coroner's jury but said he was counselled to do it *'by that wicked woman'*, who of course utterly denied the charge. Both were committed to Stafford Gaol until the next assizes.

At his trial he refused to plead. All that the court could get out of him was that he would be tried by God, upon which the judge *'caused his thumbs to be ty'd fast together with whipcord and likewise his fingers and so convey'd to gaol...'*

The following Monday he was called before the judge several times, but he consistently refused to answer. On Tuesday he was again called several times and still refused to plead, so the judge ordered him to suffer peine forte et dure.

'... and the same day he was pressed being very willing to die freely acknowledging that he deserved it, he was very penitent yet went with courage down stares to the places appointed for execution undressed himself presently and lay'd himself down willingly, without any compulsion, for the executioner to do his office which was done accordingly.'

Nathaniel's resolution in carrying out his plans refused to waver, even under the most extreme pressure.